Rails in the Canadian Rockies

Revised Pictorial Edition

Adolf Hungry Wolf

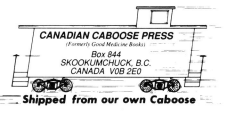

CANADIAN CABOOSE PRESS
(Formerly Good Medicine Books)
Box 844
SKOOKUMCHUCK, B.C.
CANADA V0B 2E0

Shipped from our own Caboose

Contents

(Left) Locomotive Hostler Bill Straga leans proudly from the cab of a C.P.R. 2-10-4 "Selkirk" at Field, B.C. in 1952.

(Opposite) Thundering westbound out of Field during the final season of steam in the Canadian Rockies, September 1952.
Both photos, Rail Photo Service/AHW Collection

© 1993 by Adolf Hungry Wolf
All Rights Reserved
No part of this book may be used or reproduced
without written permission from the publisher,
except in the case of brief quotations
used in reviews.
Book design - Adolf Hungry Wolf
Typesetting and Layout - Communications Plus
Colour Separations - United Graphics, Calgary
Printed and bound in Canada by Friesen Printers
First Printing - 1993
ISBN 0-920698-31-X

Published by Canadian Caboose Press
Box 844
Skookumchuck, B.C.
V0B 2E0

Preface

The original edition of this book has been long out of print, its plates destroyed. Therefore this revision is actually a new book, with some photos left out and others added.

Among the people and institutions who contributed to the assembling of these photographs and tales are the following, in no particular order: Canadian Pacific Corporate Archivist Omer S. Lavallee and his staff, including James Shields, Cecil Halsey, Dave Jones and Peter Hryzaj. British Columbia Provincial Archives; Glenbow-Alberta Institute; Archives of the Canadian Rockies; Fort Steele Museum Library; Canadian Museum of Rail Travel Archives; Lethbridge Public Library; and the Windermere Valley Historical Association Library.

Special thanks go to the following photographers, who often put great effort into capturing these historic scenes, though rewards are usually limited to printed credit lines, plus the satisfaction of accomplishment. They include: Will C. Whittaker; Ronald V. Nixon; Fred Hust; W.R. Hooper; Grant B. Will; Warren Rohn; K.C. Baker; John Poulsen; C.R. Littlebury; G.L. Moorhouse, Warren E. Miller/Railway Negative Exchange; Dick George and Al Patterson.

In a separate category is Nicholas Morant, the official Canadian Pacific photographer for over 50 years, who not only took most of the best C.P.R. photos, but also got paid for doing so.

Front cover painting by Marshall Lear
Back cover photograph by Nicholas Morant, from Canadian Pacific Corporate Archives.

PASSENGER TRAIN IN LO

Introduction

The mere mention of the Canadian Rockies brings forth vivid images in the minds of people all over the world: Lofty crags of stone towering over 10,000 feet into the sky; big-antlered elk and moose wandering through hidden forests and clear mountain streams; icy waterfalls tumbling into trout-filled pools, with bubbling hot springs nearby.

Among those who know anything of railroading, the Canadian Rockies also bring forth thoughts of long trains and mighty locomotives; steep grades and tunnels that twist over themselves; impressive stations built of logs and stones, with massive tourist hotels nearby; constant battles with deep snows, raging rivers and the threat of avalanches. It has taken tough men and mighty equipment to roll trains through the Canadian Rockies these past one hundred-plus years.

The region covered by this book forms a rough rectangle,

beginning with the prairie city of Calgary, heading west over the C.P.R. mainline through Banff, Lake Louise and the famous Spiral Tunnels. From the Kicking Horse River at Golden we head south through the Columbia and Kootenay Valleys, past Lake Windermere and historic Fort Steele, pausing at Cranbrook to explore some connecting branches. Heading east over CP's secondary mainline through the Crow's Nest Pass, we pause at Fernie and Fort Macleod on our way to Lethbridge, from where our route crosses North America's biggest railway bridge before heading north through several prairie ranching towns and back to Calgary.

Although regular passenger trains no longer serve any of the lines in this book, freight trains continue to polish the rails, providing subjects for dramatic photographs and assuring that there will be more histories written about them in the future.

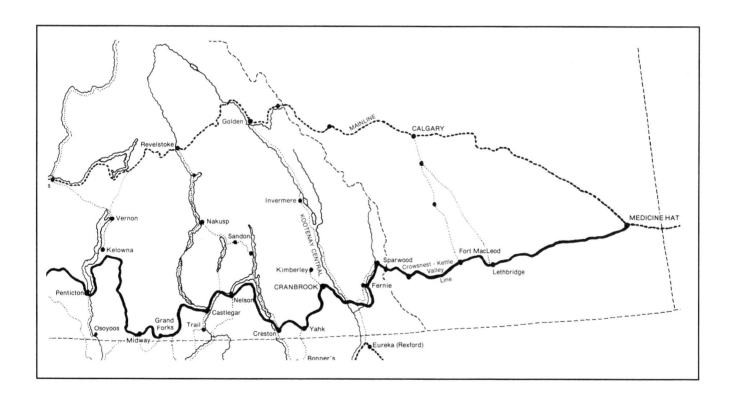

(Above) Map showing rails in the Canadian Rockies and connections.   Drawing by Garry A. Anderson

(Opposite) The grandeur of railroading in the Canadian Rockies during the first years, with a 9-car C.P.R. train paused along the lower Kicking Horse Canyon near Golden, B.C.

Vancouver Public Library Photo 31054

Selecting a Route Through the Rockies

For ten years Canada's first transcontinental rail line was planned to cross the Rockies via Yellowhead Pass, due west of Edmonton and some 150 miles further north than the route finally selected. Calgary, Banff, and Golden were nothing-places on the maps of that time, and might have remained so if the proposed northern route had actually been built. Instead, a major change of plans in May of 1881 served as a combined birth announcement for those three well-known places, along with many others that came to life with the building of the railroad.

Canadian Pacific Railway records of the early years do not give any clear reason for the change of plans. The northern route was selected after ten years of mountain explorations and the inspection of seven potential passes. It had already been surveyed by the time the Canadian government turned its rail-building project over to private hands in 1881. George Stephen became the first president of the private company, assisted by Richard Angus and James Hill, a name well-known in rail histories on both sides of the border. Hill surprised and angered many when he made the public announcement in these words:

"Gentlemen, we will cross the prairie and go by the Bow Pass (Kicking Horse) if we can get that way."

History gives us the following as major reasons why the rail line was moved south:

1. The vast prairie lands of the south offered much more arable land than the bush country further north. More arable land meant more settlers and more agriculture, which meant more money in land sales and railroad business. Originally it was thought that this region was too much like a desert to be arable.

2. A transcontinental route as far north as Edmonton would leave the lower part of Canada without Canadian rail service, and thus open for exploitation by the various American rail companies that were already looking into this potential.

3. The northern route would allow the natural resources of the southern regions to be easily removed to the U.S. Of particular concern were the vast coal deposits in Southern Alberta and the Crow's Nest Pass region, as well as the potential for lumbering and mining in those areas. With the valleys running north and south, even the geography encouraged transportation southward, across the line.

4. It has also been said that the early rail tycoons preferred to build their rail line where little settlement had taken place, so that they could be in control of such settlement. Certainly, wherever the new rail line went, most of the settling took place close by.

The route through Kicking Horse Pass was explored for a summer by the C.P.R.'s American "Railway Pathfinder," Major A.B. Rogers, a man who seems to be as famous in history books for his small stature and large vocabulary of profanities as for his rail pathfindings, which included the rugged pass through the Selkirk Mountains which bears his name, Rogers Pass. Rogers announced to his bosses that he thought the route feasible, though it had not yet been surveyed. Among his bosses was a newcomer, William Van Horne, who was no less shrewd and determined of a man than any other rail tycoon of the era. It was he who made public the decision to build through Kicking Horse Pass instead of the Yellowhead, even before the required government approval had been given.

Because the western mountain ranges all run north and south, traffic generally moved in that direction, too, until the transcontinental railroad was built. Even the survey crew that located the eventual rail route arrived at the beginning of their work in the Rocky Mountains via the famed north-south wagon road that ran to Fort Calgary from Fort Benton, in Montana Territory.

The C.P.R. survey party reached Fort Benton by steamboat in the spring of 1881. It was a sizeable party: One hundred men; nine large, covered wagons; twenty-four teams of horses; and nearly a hundred pack animals to carry equipment and supplies. The trip north took three weeks. Today, of course, it can be driven in less than a day.

On its way north the survey party passed through such future C.P.R. rail-line locations as Lethbridge, Fort Macleod, and High River. The first was then known as Coalbank, a place with few pretensions beyond some surrounding homesteads, a trading post that stayed in business mostly because of the nearby Blood Indians, and some very limited coal mining operations along the banks of the Oldman River. High River had even fewer pretensions, with only a single trading post of logs that was patronized by some settlers along with wandering groups of Stoney Indians. Only Fort Macleod showed future promise with its Mounted Police post, from which the fabled Mounties kept watch on the nearby Bloods, their Peigan relatives, and the numerous traders and whiskey peddlers that tried to cash in on the naivity of the native groups. It was the last year for the Bloods to have a successful buffalo hunt. As if in preparation for the coming of the modern ways - spearheaded by the rail line - the vast herds of buffalo disappeared from the prairies within just a few short seasons.

(Above) The new Canadian Pacific Railway roadbed can be seen in the foreground of this 1884 view of the Canadian Rockies. On the slope above, a traffic jam on the old wagon road that connected the prairies with British Columbia before the rails came.   Canadian Pacific Corporate Archives

Building The Line

"For some of us are bums, for whom work has no charms,
And some of us are farmers, a-working for our farms,
But all are jolly fellows, who come from near and far,
To work up in the Rockies on the C.P.R."

So went a popular song among construction workers who layed tracks over the Rocky Mountains, according to British writer Morley Roberts. Himself a member of the construction gang, Roberts went beyond the anonymity of most rail workers by describing his Canadian experiences in a book, (*The Western Avenues*, London, 1887), and by having a station stop named after him. The stop, Morley, Alberta, has become the home base of the main branch of the mountain-dwelling Stoney Tribe.

Track laying had continued towards the mountains right after the line reached Calgary in the summer of 1883. From the townsite to the beginning of Kicking Horse Pass the rails were layed as easily as they had been across the level prairies. At one point the construction gang beat the world track-laying record, which had been six hundred feet in six and a half minutes. One six hundred foot section of the C.P.R. was layed down in just under five minutes.

During the winter the track-laying stopped, and all but 500 men were laid off. Those who were kept at work spent the cold season cutting half a million ties and twenty thousand cords of fuel for the wood burning locomotives. Construction headquarters were located at the place where track-laying had stopped for the winter, a place known today as Lake Louise. The camp that surrounded the headquarters became known as Holt City, in honor of the man who ran the company store there. Later the name of the place was changed to Laggan, and finally Lake Louise, by which name it has become a famous tourist destination.

The serious part of building the rail line over the Rockies began in 1884 as soon as winter pulled back enough to allow the workers to start. The C.P.R. put out a call for

7

twelve thousand workmen, which was probably a far larger group than all the people would make who had seen that part of the Rockies up till then. Morley Roberts described the effect of this huge mob on the mountain wilderness:

"Round me, I saw the primaeval forest torn down, cut and hewed and hacked, pine and cedar and hemlock. Here and there lay piles of ties, and near them, closely stacked, thousands of rails. The brute power of man's organized civilization had fought with nature and had for the time vanquished her. Here lay the trophies of the battle."

If ties and rails were considered trophies of the battle to build the rail line over the Rockies, what would we call all the other side-products that invaded the land along with the great hordes of men. What about the forest fires started by careless crews, that were said to have made the skies smokey from the mountain summits clear to the Columbia River and beyond. What about the trash and garbage left behind by such a hurried crowd? What about the dynamited mountain faces, the scalped forests, and the trampled meadows and streams? The men were too busy working, and when they were off work they either slept, or they spent their hard-earned money in the countless illegal saloons, gambling places, and houses of pleasure that followed the construction camps just like the trails of garbage.

(Below) C.P.R. No. 145, an old-time 4-4-0, was photographed near the summit of the Rockies in 1884 with flat cars used to haul construction supplies.

Glenbow-Alberta Institute

(Above) **Turn-of-the-century at the outpost station of Kananaskis, Alberta.**

Kananaskis

"Approaching Kananaskis (Alt. 4,100 ft., 54 miles from Calgary) the mountains suddenly appear close at hand and seemingly an impenetrable barrier, their bases deeply tinted in purple, and their sides flecked with white and gold, while high above, dimly outlined in the mists, are distant snowy peaks. The Kananaskis River is crossed by a high iron bridge, a little above where it joins the Bow, and the roar of the great falls of the Bow (called Kananaskis Falls) may be heard from the railway. The mountains now rise abruptly in great masses, streaked and capped with snow and ice, and just beyond Kananaskis station a bend in the line brings the train between two almost vertical walls of dizzy height. This is the gap by which the Rocky Mountains are entered."   From a C.P.R. Tour Guide of the 1880's

(Below) **Early days on the C.P.R. in the Rockies, with a well-dressed crew aboard vintage track speeders. Faces are serious in spite of the clown, who is leaning on the "signal box" of a primitve stub switch.**

Archives of the Canadian Rockies

Working the Calgary - Banff Way Freight in the Late 1920's

By Clayton Harris

"I have often worked the way freights between Calgary and Banff - as a fireman in the Twenties and Thirties, later as an engineer. I always enjoyed working west out of Calgary because this line had good equipment and the mountain water was best for the steam engines. In addition, the scenery is very wonderful and there was lots of wildlife to watch for.

We generally started at seven in the morning. I would get my call for the job two hours earlier, which was enough time to prepare food and clothing, since I would be away from home overnight. Before I was married I used to take the streetcar down as far as the Brewery and walk from there over to the Alyth roundhouse. We booked in at the office there. In those days our motive power was usually one of the D-10 4-6-0's that handled most of the way freights and mixed trains. The engine would be all ready for us by the time we arrived at Alyth, having been serviced by the wipers.

Our first job was often to switch the refrigerator cars at Keith, where the C.P.R. had an ice house. The ice was taken out of the river in big chunks, after the river was frozen to about two feet thickness. The ice was stored all year long. There were ice houses in Calgary and Banff, in addition to Keith. The one in Calgary was at Alyth, and it was a big one - about 20 to 30 car lengths. The Reefers were pulled up and filled at both ends, leaving the middle for loading with perishable goods. In the winter we often spent 3 to 4 hours switching ice cars at Keith.

Our next stop for switching was Cochrane, where they handled all kinds of freight, as usual in a small town of its size. Past Cochrane was the oil spur at Mitford. A switcher went out there from Calgary and worked the oil plant, so the way freight only picked up the cars that were already set out for it.

The next place we worked was Morley, on the Stoney Indian Reserve. There was usually quite a bit of switching to do here. We brought in box cars of goods for the agency. The Indians had a sawmill and we picked up car loads of fence posts from it. We also handled stock and feed for the tribe. The company had a gravel pit at Morley from which we got carloads of track ballast and some commercial gravel.

West of Morley is Seebe, where we used to do some switching for the large boys camp that was run by the YMCA. The next place was Kananaskis where they worked lime. After that came Exshaw, with cement; Canmore, with coal; and then Banff, where we handled all kinds of freight. By the time we finished switching and got ready to tie up for the night it was often close to midnight.

The engineer and fireman slept in the C.P.R. bunkhouse, across the tracks from the Banff station. The train crew, of course, slept in their caboose. They cooked their meals in the caboose, too, while we generally cooked ours in the engine. How we cooked depended on the kind of food we had with us. For instance, in the mornings we would cook our bacon and eggs on top of a layer of hot coals that we took out of the engine's firebox with the scoop shovel. If we wanted baked potatoes, later on, we would lay them up on the steam dome, by the pop valves, in the morning. We used to carry a galvanized pot for cooking stew and so on. This we would set up at the location where the main steam pipe enters the locomotive cab and is distributed to such places as the inspirator. That's a very hot spot, and it didn't take long for the food to cook. Sometimes we cooked steaks or pork chops up there, as well. In the winter, when it was really cold, we would wrap some waste rags around the cook pots to keep them warm.

The following morning we were generally called for 6 a.m. The way we worked it was to get most of the switching done on the way to Banff, so that we could roll right along back to Calgary and get there by the middle of the day. Of course, it was downhill to Calgary, so we didn't have to work the engine very much either. We took water at Cochrane, Morley, Canmore, and Banff. In Canmore we also took coal, which lasted up to Banff and back.

Elk and deer were the animals that I used to see most often, along the way to Banff. West of Exshaw there used to be a place we called the Gap Curve, where the speed limit was down to 20 mph. That was a good place to see wildlife. I remember one winter coming along there and seeing a big band of mountain sheep near the tracks. The engineer had to whistle for the curve, and in so doing he scared the sheep into running. One ran underneath a big rock on top of which was a mountain lion lying in wait. Our whistle didn't scare him at all. One of the sheep ran under that rock, and the cougar jumped on its back and killed it with one bite through the neck."

(Above) No. 5911 thunders into Field, B.C. on a "seaboard freight" in September 1937.

AHW Collection

(no 4) STATION. COCHRANE. ALBERTA.

(Above) A westbound freight train is pulled up by the Cochrane station around 1920, while its 2-8-2 locomotive takes water.
(Below) A passenger train at Exshaw in April, 1945. Both Photos, Canadian Pacific Corporate Archives

(Above) Late afternoon light bathes an extra east approaching Exshaw during 1941.

(Below) Hooping up a "19" order to highballing train No. 952, heading through Exshaw on its way to Calgary in 1946.

All Five Photos, G.L. Moorhouse

(Top) It was a sunny day in the winter of 1946 as C.P.R. train No. 951 rumbled westbound past the station at Exshaw, Alberta.

(Centre) A westbound freight behind Mikado 5432, as seen from the Exshaw station platform in 1942.

(Below) Somebody has got some explaining to do with the superintendent, though probably not this dapper engineer from the looks of him. No. 564 is "on the ground" at Exshaw in 1941.

(Above) Banff station around 1910, with horse-drawn carriages meeting passengers coming from wooden cars. Glenbow-Alberta Institute

Banff

"Banff - Alt. 4,500 ft. 82 miles past Calgary. Station for Rocky Mountain Park and the Hot Springs - a medical watering-place and pleasure resort. This park is a national reservation, 26 m. long N.E. and S.W. by 10 m. wide, embracing parts of the valleys of the Bow, Spray and Cascade Rivers, Devil's Lake and several noble mountain ranges. No part of the Rockies exhibits a greater variety of sublime and pleasing scenery; and nowhere are good points of view and features of special interest so accessible, since many good roads and bridle paths have been made. The railway station at Banff is in the midst of impressive mountains. The huge mass northward is Cascade Mt. (9,875 ft.); eastward is Mt. Inglismaldie, and the heights of the Fairholme sub-range, behind which lies Devil's Lake. Still further eastward the sharp cone of Peechee (in that range) closes the view in that direction; this is the highest mountain visible, exceeding 10,000 ft. To the left of Cascade Mt. and just north of the track rises the wooded ridge of Squaw Mt., beneath which lie the Vermillion lakes, seen just after leaving the station. Up the Bow, westward, tower the distant, snowy, central heights of the Main range about Simpson's Pass, most prominently the square, wall-like crest of Mt. Massive. A little nearer, at the left, is seen the northern end of the Bourgeau range, and still nearer, the Sulphur Mt., along the base of which are the Hot Springs. The isolated bluff southward is Tunnel Mt., while just behind the station, Rundle Peak rises sharply, so near at hand as to cut off all the view in that direction. The village of Banff is one and one half miles southwest of the station, on the other side of the Bow. A steel bridge takes the carriage-road across to the magnificent hotel, built by the railway company, near the fine falls in the Bow and the mouth of the rapid Spray River. This hotel, which has every modern convenience and luxury including baths supplied from the hot sulfur springs, is kept open from 15th May to 1st October, and thither people from all lands flock in numbers. It is most favorably placed for health, picturesque views, and as a centre for canoeing, driving, walking or mountain climbing. There are also a sanitorium and hospital in the village, and a museum of more than local interest has been established by the Government. Trout of extraordinary size occur in Devil's lake, and deep trolling for these affords fine sport. Wild Sheep (the bighorn) and mountain goats are occasionally to be seen on the neighboring heights. The springs are at different elevations upon the eastern slope of Sulphur Mt., the highest being 900 ft. above the Bow. All are reached by fine roads, commanding glorious landscapes. The more important springs have been improved by the Government, and picturesque bathing houses have been erected and placed under the care of attendants. In one locality is a pool inside a dome-roofed cave, entered by an artificial tunnel; and near by, another spring forms an open basin of warm, sulfurous water. Since the opening of the railway, these springs have been largely visited, and testimony to their wonderful curative properties is plentiful."

From a C.P.R. Tour Guide of the 1880's

(Above) Ten-wheeler No. 591 was a regular for many years on passenger trains through Banff, such as this westbound pulling up to the station in 1915.   Canadian Pacific Corporate Archives

(Above) "The Dominion," Canada's premier train, pulls into Banff on a wintry day in 1950, headed east behind mighty "Selkirk" locomotive No. 5921.

Rail Photo Service/AHW Collection

(Above) Westbound Train No. 3 sits at the Banff Station on May 22, 1946, behind Selkirk No. 5923.

R.V. Nixon Photo

(Below) The town-side of Banff station in August 1947, awaiting the next crowd of passengers.

W.C. Whittaker Photo

Above) A westbound passenger train is seen in the late 1940s arriving at Banff station behind No. 5924. Trains still rumble past this historic building though its interior now serves as a fine-food restaurant.

Nicholas Morant Photo/Canadian Pacific Corporate Archives

(Above) Freight and passenger meet at Banff in September of 1943 as the westbound "Dominion" comes charging towards the station behind No. 5927 while the crew of No. 2355 waits to head for Calgary.

Paterson-George Collection

(Below) For 30 years passenger trains coming to Banff included dome cars on "The Canadian," seen here in the summer of 1978.

AHW Photo

(Above) Chateau Lake Louise and its tramway. Victoria Glacier is in the background

The Mountain Resorts

"The mountain where the water falls," was what local Stoney Indians called Cascade Mountain, beneath which Banff had its beginnings. At that time there was no national park. Most of those who headed for the area were looking at possibilities for mineral developments, not for tourist industry. The original townsite was some distance from the present one, near the area where the buffalo herd now roams. The place was called "Siding 29."

Twenty miles west of Banff was the mining town of Silver City. With a peak population of 3,000 it threatened, for a while, to become a more important place than Calgary. Today, only a few signs remain of this short-lived community. But when the rail line reached there in 1883, it was important enough to have its own station.

In 1887 parliament changed the future course of that re-gion by designating it as the Rocky Mountains Park of Canada and restricting all developments within its boundaries. Plans were made for a new townsite called Banff, as well as for the construction of a public sanitorium at the nearby hot springs. In 1889 the C.P.R. completed the first version of its Banff Springs Hotel, which has become known as one of the foremost mountain resorts in the world.

The Banff Springs Hotel became a destination point for many passengers on C.P.R. trains into the mountains. It suffered from fires and other problems as the years went by, so that the C.P.R. completely rebuilt it in the latter 1920's. Most of the new construction was out of native stone quarried from nearby Mt. Rundle, then trimmed with Tyndal stone brought from Manitoba. After rebuilding, it was 500 feet long, consisting of a central tower 12 stories high and two wings of 8 stories each. Accommodations were made for 1,100 guests using 600 bedrooms. Baths could be filled with water piped right from the hot springs. Temperatures of this water vary from 78 to 115 degrees, Fahrenheit.

At Lake Louise the C.P.R. built another tremendous resort hotel, beginning with a chalet in 1890. This was rebuilt and enlarged in 1893, and at various times since then. A narrow gauge tramway was built from the railroad station to Chateau Lake Louise in 1912. The 3-1/2 mile line went up an average grade of 3.3% through a series of switchbacks, with a passing siding half-way up and turning loops at each end. Six different rail cars were used on the line, all of them powered by gasoline engines. Each car held about 40 passengers, except for the two with flat decks that were built for hauling baggage and freight. Clayton Harris says there used to be four or five of these cars waiting at the station each time a passenger train came in. The men who ran them were called Motormen. They were C.P.R. employees, but hired through the hotel, not the railway offices. He says their job was comparable to driving a bus. In the winter time there wasn't much traffic for them, but they were used regularly to bring up coal and groceries for the hotel employees. The line was closed after the 1930 season and the equipment scrapped.

(Below) An open tramway car with a trailer for baggage is seen crossing a bridge over the Bow River headed for Chateau Lake Louise around 1920. Byron Harmon Photo/Archives of the Canadian Rockies

(Above) An early view of the Laggan Station, before it became Lake Louise. This building is now in Calgary's Heritage Park.

(Below) No. 5924 pulls up to Lake Louise Station with the westbound "Dominion" in 1936.

Both photos, Canadian Pacific Corporate Archives

(Above) A helper engine waits outside Lake Louise station on this cold January day in 1948. Since passenger service ended here in 1990, this historic building has become a noteworthy restaurant.

Paterson-George Collection

Lake Louise

"Laggan - Alt. 4,930 ft. 116 miles from Calgary. At Laggan the railway leaves the Bow and ascends a tributary from the west, which courses through a gap in the Bow range. Looking upward through this gap towards Bow Lake and the huge peak of Mt. Hector, a view is obtained of the first of the great glaciers. It is a broad, crescent-shaped river of ice, the further end concealed behind the lofty yellow cliffs that hem it in. It is 1,300 feet above you, and a dozen miles away. Laggan is the station for the Lakes in the Clouds. Ponies and vehicles are here in waiting for tourists intending to visit these picturesque and interesting lakes, which, perched on the mountains' sides amidst the most romantic environments, are rare gems whose loveliness and charm surpass all description. Lake Louise, which is the first, is two and one-half miles from the station by a pleasant carriage drive across the face of the mountain. On the margin of the beautiful lake there is a comfortable Chalet hotel, where parties take luncheon, or, if any desire to stay over, accommodation is provided..."

From a C.P.R. Tour Guide of the 1880's

Crossing the Rockies in the Locomotive Cab

"Thrill-Charged Scenes of Mountains Look Different from Front End"

(Excerpts from July-August 1924 edition of *The Canadian White Ribbon Tidings*)

By A.R. Pinci

"Accompanied by mighty sternutations of smoke, steam that had coursed through the elaborate veinwork of the locomotive began to move the heavy transcontinental train westward. The bell ceased jangling, nodding to and fro silently on its pivots as though in recognition of its inadequacy in the midst of a confusion of noises. Snorts and wheezes, at first disconnected and discordant, attuned themselves as forward motion became accelerated, and presently subsided into an opaque echo of new but decipherable sounds - that of metal on metal, metal against metal.

And then began our dance - that of the fireman and myself, each pivoting on either or both feet, as a lateral swaying forced us out of equilibrium. The engineer, resting easily on his perch, a hand skillfully caressing the air-brake lever, watched ahead - a blur in the foreground, because the day was cloudy and mists hung low, fringing mountain tops and pines emerging amid their loftiness, the track visible in sections as we twined our way along a serpentine maze, skirting here a tiny torrential stream, crossing there a barren rocky bed, but always contesting a difficult grade, first upward and then downward.

A sheer drop of 1,900 feet in 12 miles, through baby canyons above high valleys, through spiral tunnels - two of them - at one time a panoramic vista of many miles beneath us, for either of us could have stepped into eternity during any of those 55 miles of arduous piloting. That was a sensation that I felt as I rode on the engine, but that I missed when I made the trip safely and comfortably ensconced on the rear platform of the observation car.

For this is what I wanted to know - what of the road ahead, as it met the eye, instead of the road behind, as it disappeared from sight. There is always a difference between meeting a thing and leaving that thing behind, and I wanted to see what the engineer saw - that which the most timid passenger even fails to think about while gazing upon scenes of panoramic grandeur that have been rendered safe by man's engineering skill.

There was no time or thought for scenery forward. It was the same view that travelers 300 or 400 feet behind us would soon gaze upon; the same towering peaks, the unkempt hanging gardens, the same streams, the same bridges, the same crumbling cuts, but we approached with care, that which passengers soon after greeted with enthusiastic carelessness...

Of course, the officials of the Canadian Pacific Railroad did not favor my request for this ride. It was all very well a few years ago 'When trains plodded along a few miles an hour', but at higher speed - well the risk was too great ...

Permission was finally granted. The station master at Banff gave me a paper to sign. The dream of childhood abides in grown-up days, and not one of the fellow passengers who knew about my reportorial task, either before or after, but did not wish to 'try it some time'...

If the officials did not welcome my proposal, I confess that it was nothing in comparison to the engineer and the fireman, each of whom read and reread the formal and official authorization to 'hang around', furtively looked at me, looked me over, and wondered.

On board it was up to me. They offered no encouragement. I stood upon the laminated steel floor that bridges tender and locomotive itself, where despite my poor terpsichorean skill, I was obliged to try steps and humps that must have been quite funny, only I couldn't see them ... When you are not wanted, those present don't mind letting you know it, and as I reached out a hand ... happened to rest two fingers - fortunately not more than two - upon the six-foot poker which only a few moments before had been flirting with the sizzling coals, and I realized quite painfully that interrupting any flirtation is dangerous business, especially when it is so logical as that of poker and fire. I could not stand upright anywhere; first, because there was no place to stand, and second, because I didn't care to dance anyway. Besides, we had covered five or six miles by now - I could tell because Castle Mountain was becoming more castellated - and if I wanted something to write about I'd better find myself a perch.

If at any time locomotive-riding will be made a popular outdoor sport let us hope that the powers that be will provide suitable perches, at least provide one. For there was not even one. Moreover, I did not like the frequent hot blasts emanating from the grate as the bisected gravity doors swung apart in response to the fireman's left foot on an operating lever. I had to think quickly, too, because the latter presently began to water the coal dust, the dampened boards steaming unpleasantly. This time I put out my right hand - and, of course, I got it nicely wetted, for the water-tank had rid itself of its over fullness. I tried a lateral hand-bar and this time it was nicely smeared with soot...

...I looked for a foothold...and we had yet 47 miles to Field - I wondered as to the best method of using my surplus leg for the time being.

...I was outside the cab, behind the engineer, something like half a yard below his level and anatomically projecting into the outer space in defiance of all. I saw what the engineer saw and what he did not see. I peered down and under - and there were the tireless drivers and their regular metallic resonance born of their thrusts, and there is something unusually hypnotizing about this marvelous movement. Coming upon each curve, one feels forward the momentum that is lost in the rear - and yet despite the eye's illusion that no train could successfully negotiate the curve ahead and remain on the track, there we are - riding over them as a steel flange caresses steel head. Unless the curve is unusually sharp its existence is almost unnoticeable...

Well, to make a now 40-mile story a 20 mile one, I made the fireman understand that if I was a poor one at railroading I was a fair one at pencil-pushing. Magic of Magic! The sun beaming upon the earth after the deluge never brightened things as that smile of (Brotherhood of Locomotive Engineers and Firemen) Brother F. England. It saved an extra shovelful of coal, things warmed up so quickly. And by now it was a better appreciated smile, because he had shoveled something like three tons of bituminous coal (and a poor grade of it, which means more coal) into the firebox, shaken two of six grates, washed that hot floor twice, crushed lumpy fuel with a small sledge, watched the water gauge, taken on water, filled his pipe twice, nibbled at a quick lunch, and a few other things. But despite all this, and doing it all over again, more or less, he managed to show me the points of interest, from Mt. Hector to the Great Divide and farther.

There must have been some high sign exchanged between Brother England and Engineer Monilaws - J.G. - because the latter, too, at once had something to say. I did my best, trying to balance myself on the swaying platform, left-facing when the fireman addressed me and right-facing when the boss spoke...

We reached Lake Louise. We had risen 510 feet, and were now 5,044 feet above sea level. Here a powerful oil-burner was coupled to our locomotive for the coming rise - a few hundred feet up to Stephen, almost a mile vertically from Montreal, my starting point.

The run between Stephen and Field is essentially simple, but it is delicate. That is, it is simple so far as the train itself goes, because gravity makes motion, but the strain on the engineer is intensified. The sense of hearing governs him, since he can see nothing.

At Field I left two most genial men. As I wended back to my stuffy sleeping car they detached No. 564, as this was the end of their division run. Later that evening they would go back - retrace their route."

(Below) One of the most spectacular places to see trains in the Canadian Rockies is between Lake Louise and Banff, under the 9,030 foot peak of Castle Mountain. This picture shows the eastbound "Dominion" led in 1947 by Mikado (2-8-2) No 5429, when the engine was just four years old.

Nicholas Morant Photo/Canadian Pacific Corporate Archives

Spiral Tunnels and "The Big Hill"

Eastbound trains on the mainline out of Field have to tackle the "Big Hill," which has the steepest grade and sharpest curves of any mainline in Canada. In fact, until the Spiral Tunnels were built in 1910 to reduce the grade, the Big Hill was the steepest piece of mainline track in the world.

Construction crews of the transcontinental line reached this part of the Rockies in the 1880's. At that time C.P.R. President Van Horne said it would take an extra year just to drill enough tunnels to make the grade on the Big Hill conform to government requirements, which called for a maximum of 2.2 percent. He managed to get government approval to push the line through at 4.4 percent, twice that allowed. The understanding was that this would be a temporary situation to expedite completion of the mainline, only. But it was over 20 years before the line was rebuilt. During that time this 8-mile section was the most difficult and expensive to operate on the whole Canadian Pacific Railway.

The first engines to work on the Big Hill were tiny, early-model 4-4-0's and 4-6-0's and some light 2-8-0's. These engines had no air pumps for brakes, but instead had to rely on the engineer reversing their drivers and the fireman tightening a handbrake on the tender. Those thin wheels against thin rails on a 4.4 percent grade often created a situation similar to holding an ice cube still on top of a mirror.

The challenging conditions of the Big Hill forced the C.P.R. to adopt some unusual railway operations. For instance, this short stretch of track was the only independent block on the mainline. A special trainmaster at Field was in charge of every train going up or down the Big Hill. At each end of his short domain the trains ran by the system-wide train order network. But on the Big Hill they ran by his special orders, only.

One of the more unusual mishaps that this trainmaster had to deal with involved a missing snowplow. During a heavy blizzard in the winter of 1900, an engine was sent up the hill from Field pushing a snowplow to clear the line. Inside the snowplow were seven men, as well as a load of spikes to weigh down the plow. The weather was so bad that the engineer and fireman could hardly see anything. When they entered the first tunnel the engine's headlight lit the way ahead - but there was no snowplow. Neither man in the cab could figure out what might have happened to it. They backed out of the tunnel and toward Field, expecting to see it somewhere off the tracks. But when they got to Field without seeing it, they began to wonder if they had even left with it in the first place. Inside the station they were assured that they had.

With extra searchers aboard, the men again took their engine uphill out of Field to look for the missing plow and its crew. Just before the tunnel they found the conductor, struggling through deep drifts of snow. He said the plow had jumped the tracks and gone some 300 feet down the side of the mountain to the riverbank below. Fortunately no one had been injured, although he had fallen out of the plow's cupola on the way down.

(Below) A snowplow at work on the Big Hill. It was made of wood and completely hand operated by crews who often had difficulty seeing where they were going. AHW Collection

Snow Plow, Field, B. C.

C.P.R. Passenger Train, Canadian Rockies

(Above) "Climbing the Big Hill" is the subject of this turn-of-the-century post-card published by Valentine & Sons. One of the escape ramps is on the right.

Good Medicine Foundation

The Big Hill soon earned itself a reputation that was sometimes more spectacular than the actual events. For instance, an English professor named G.G. Ramsey wrote the following account, with the title, *"Over the Rocky Mountains by the Canadian Pacific Line in 1884."*

"Once a train, with 270 men going down for their day's work, broke loose. One by one, all the men jumped off. Scarce had the last man leapt, when the train, rushing at forty or fifty miles an hour down the new-laid track, and scorning a side line up the hill turned open to intercept the runaway, 'jumped' the rails at the curve close to the second crossing of the river, and dashed straight on into a precipitous face of rock. 'There was just enough iron left,' said the pointsman who saw the crash, 'to fill a moderate sized wheelbarrow.'"

Locomotive shop crews were no doubt capable engine rebuilders, but not from parts left in a wheelbarrow. C.P.R. records show that all engines used during construction survived intact and went on working for a number of years more. But the possibilities for such a disastrous wreck caused the installation of three emergency sidings, each of them leading steeply uphill for enough distance to stop run-

away trains, and each of them constantly manned by a watchman.

In addition to the emergency exits, speed limits were kept very low, with passenger trains allowed eight miles an hour and freight trains six. Before going down the hill, every train had to stop so that its brakes and sanding gear could be checked. On the way down, brakemen had to drop off and inspect the train's wheels as they went by to look for sliding and overheating. On freight cars the brakemen walked along the roofs and used special wooden clubs to tighten each brake wheel as much as possible.

Unfortunately, traffic on the C.P.R. has always been heavier on westbound trains than on those headed east. Thus, the downhill trains were more frequently loaded than those going uphill. Uphill the battle was mainly one of putting enough engines on the train. Most uphill trains were short, but required four locomotives. Some went up with five or six. The special train that carried the Duke and Duchess of Cornwall and York (later King George V and Queen Mary), in 1902, had nine passenger cars and five locomotives. By this time the trains were equipped with air brakes.

(Above) No. 314 on the turntable at Field. Nick Morant says this engine blew up on Field Hill when the crew allowed the crown sheet to go dry. His wife's grandfather was the engineer, and he died in this explosion. Canadian Pacifiic-Corporate Archives

In the early years all traffic on the Big Hill was handled by special "hill crews". They used four heavy Consolidation (2-8-0) engines that were permanently based in Field. Regular freight crews would handle their trains as far as Field, or Laggan (now Lake Louise), depending on which way they were headed. There they would turn their engines and head back to where they came from with another train, while the "hill crew" took the train over the section in between. In the case of passenger trains the regular crews worked clear through from Medicine Hat to Donald. At the top of the Big Hill they would cut off their trains and run down to Field with only their engines. The hill crew would bring the train down to Field behind them, from where they continued. Eastbound passenger crews stayed at the head of their train, but got hill crews with pushers from behind.

Laggan and Field both had boxcars as their original stations. The area was part of a huge Western Division that went from Donald, B.C. clear to Port Arthur, Ontario. The mountain section was then still so remote from developed parts of Canada that the North West Mounted Police felt obliged to search all trains at Laggan for liquor smuggling and other contraband going into British Columbia and the Northwest Territories.

To cut down on unnecessary weight, early freight trains on the Big Hill had no cabooses and passenger trains had no dining cars. In order to feed hungry travellers, the C.P.R. built a pleasant restaurant and hotel at Field in 1886. Called the Mount Stephen House, it was the C.P.R.'s first hotel. In 1918 it was taken over by the YMCA and operated as a boarding house until 1954, when it was torn down. For many years it was a trackside landmark in Field.

The hill crews based in Field not only hauled trains up and down the Big Hill, they also provided pusher service to westbound trains that had to climb to the summit, three miles from Field. In 1902 that section of track was rebuilt to cut down on the grade, and after that helpers were run between Golden and Leanchoil.

Around 1910 the C.P.R. built six articulated locomotives for the Big Hill - each one with two sets of cylinders to power two sets of driving wheels under one long boiler. These Mallet-types (0-6-6-0) were hard to maintain and the old timers said they were even harder to fire, being like two units with one boiler, although their crews got a higher rate of pay which somewhat offset the extra work. By 1917 all six had been rebuilt to standard Decapod (2-10-0) types.

It would be agonizing to recount all the various runaways

28

and other accidents that happened on the Big Hill in its tough days, but it is good to know that there have been no runaway accidents since the line was rebuilt in 1910. Of course, equipment and safety features have changed tremendously since the days of putting the engine in reverse and tightening a handbrake on the tender in order to stop. Here is one example of the many drawbacks to those early methods:

At Laggan, downhill freight trains were taken over by the hill crews, with one of the trainmen riding on top of the last car, in lieu of a caboose. At night this man held a red lantern. One time a crew that was new to the Big Hill was making a light run downhill, bringing only a caboose with the trainmen aboard. The engineer and fireman got scared when their engine started to slide faster on the grade, so they jumped off and left the trainmen in their caboose. When the trainmen saw what happened they managed to uncouple the caboose from the engine and slow it down with its own handbrake. The watchman at the third safety switch heard no whistle signaling that the train was under control, so he sent the lone engine up the emergency ramp. Of course, the engine wheels all this time were going backwards, since the engineer had been trying to stop before he bailed out. When this engine got to the end of the safety track it started back in the opposite way, which began with a steep downhill run. About that time the slow-moving caboose, with the trainmen still aboard, reached the safety switch, too. When the men saw the engine coming back at them they jumped off, leaving the caboose to be badly smashed when the collision came. This kind of thing happened more than once.

Finally, in 1906 the long-expected grade rebuilding between Field and Hector was begun. It took three years of continuous work and nearly a million dollars to do the job. Several construction camps were set up at various sites. Narrow gauge tracks and equipment were used in the immediate area. Some of this equipment came from the old narrow gauge lines around Lethbridge and one of the locomotives is still at the bottom of Sink Lake, where it fell.

A spectacular result of the line's rebuilding are the two Spiral Tunnels, which have gained world-wide attention as examples of masterful engineering. Their design was based on a similar tunnel in the Swiss Alps. The company employed over one thousand men to construct the Spiral Tunnels, with work going on through all four entrances at the same time. In both cases the alignments were within inches of each other when the two ends met.

(Below) A narrow gauge construction train during the building of the Spiral Tunnels. The 2-6-0 Mogul engine still carries the number 15 from her years on the NWC&N Railway (later AR&I) out of Lethbridge. It is said that this locomotive now rests in the lake along the mainline, where it fell after the construction work ended. Note the 3-rail tracks and the standard gauge car being pulled by a horse. Canadian Pacific-Corprate Archives

(Above) An artist's sketch of the Spiral Tunnels, looking downhill towards Field.

From the entrance of the Upper Spiral Tunnel the grade drops 425 feet before reaching the exit of the Lower Spiral Tunnel, some 4.6 miles distant. Watching trains negotiate this famous section is possible from a lookout-site on the Trans-Canada Highway. Some of the scenes in the famous movie, "Doctor Zhivago", were filmed along here.

The Spiral Tunnels were planned by the C.P.R.'s senior engineer of Western lines, John E. Schwitzer, who also designed the great Viaduct at Lethbridge. Earlier plans for reducing grades on the Big Hill had called for a maze of bridges, tunnels, and fills all the way down the narrow canyon. Schwitzer eliminated the maze for the two tunnels that double over themselves. The upper one is built inside of Cathedral Mountain and is 3,255 feet long. The lower one is built across the canyon, inside of Mount Ogden, and is 2,922 feet long. Some of today's modern freight trains are even longer than that. Their engines can enter, go all the way through, exit, and pass over the entrance before the caboose begins the underground journey. There are no other tunnels like them in North America.

(Above) To symbolize tracks looping over themselves, this interesting scene was taken at the Lower Spiral Tunnel in 1948. Through a double exposure, we see both the front and back of the same passenger train.

Nicholas Morant Photo/Canadian Pacific Corporate Archives

• FIELD •

Located in beautiful Yoho National Park, Field has always been an interesting railway town. It is a division point, where crews from Alberta change trains with crews from British Columbia - one coming up from Calgary, the other from Revelstoke. In the days of steam locomotives it was a place for servicing a train's engines and adding on extra helpers. Powerful engines of the mountains filled the roundhouse stalls and the ready tracks, keeping the turntable busy.

The town was named for Cyrus Field, who laid the trans-Atlantic cable, though he didn't have much to do with mountain railway building. It was originally planned as another resort center, along the lines of Banff and Lake Louise, though it never did reach the popularity of either of those. To accommodate tourists, the C.P.R. built one of their lavish resort hotels right by the tracks. Since early mountain trains could not handle the extra weight of a dining car on the steep grades, all trains paused long enough at Field for passengers to eat at the fancy hotel, named Mount Stephen House.

(Above) Early days of railroading at Field, B.C. in the late 1880's. The cars still had link-and-pin couplers and no air brakes.

AHW Collection

(Above) Looking from the tracks at the original Field log station sometime around 1890. The bulletin board reads: "July 11 - No. 1 on Time   No. 2 on Time."

Vancouver Public Library Photo No. 885

(Above) A first-class machine of its day was Richmond Compound engine No. 671, built in 1898 and photographed soon afterwards with a proud crew at Field.   Vaux family photo/Archives of the Canadian Rockies

(Below) Vintage engines and railroad men at the Field roundhouse in 1905.

(Above) Selkirks like No. 5904 were the biggest engines based at the Field roundhouse.
(Below) Extra West 5919 leaving Field on August 13, 1939.   Both Photos, Canadian Pacific Corporate Archives

(Above) The conductor watches from the steps of his caboose as a pusher engine begins working to help an eastbound freight uphill out of Field in June of 1951.   W.C. Whittaker Photo
(Below) The "Dominion" is seen leaving Field for Golden and Vancouver in 1950, with one of the C.P.R.'s unique open-air "mountain observation" cars bringing up the rear.

Rail Photo Service/AHW Collection

(Above) In the first seasons of diesel power at Field, Train No. 8 is seen with an A-B-A set of F7's, led by No. 4069.   Rail Photo Service/AHW Collection

(Opposite) Final seasons of the Field roundhouse in the winter of 1978, by which time only a few of the stone stalls remained standing.   AHW Photo

(Below) Second No. 7 is arriving at Field behind F7 No. 4029 in September 1952.

Rail Photo Service/AHW Collection

The Mountain Memories of a Fireman

by Bert Lanning

"In 1928 I was working as a locomotive fireman on the C.P.R. out of Revelstoke. Firing steam locomotives was never dull work for me. Unusual incidents kept cropping up to make trips interesting.

One day I was sent out to Field to relieve a sick fireman on the Golden Pusher. Our work was assisting trains from Golden up the two percent grade through Kicking Horse Pass to Field. My engineer was a very friendly chap named "Windy" McClean. We were assigned to a typical pusher engine, a 2-10-2 Santa Fe Type, No. 5808. All motive power running between Revelstoke and Field was oil fired by that time, so that a fireman's job was relatively easy. Many hand-fired coal burners were then still working out of both Revelstoke and Field, but not between those two mainline points. This was because of the 5-mile long Connaught Tunnel, at Glacier.

The 5808 was a powerful engine and what we called a "free steamer," making my job enjoyable. Thundering up through Kicking Horse Pass either on the tail-end of a freight or the head-end of a passenger was a thrilling experience. Once I had the oil controls set correctly and the injector cut down for the right amount of water to feed the boiler, I could relax and enjoy the thunderous blast out of the locomotive's stack. This was like music to my ears, and my feet kept time with the 1-2-3-4 beat.

Running at the head end of a passenger train was perhaps most glamorous, but it also meant extra responsibilities. The lead engine on all doubleheaded trains is in complete charge of the trainline air. As soon as we coupled on to the train's regular engine and had our air hoses hooked up, my engineer made the mandatory standing brake test, moving the trainline brake handle over to emergency position. This resulted in a deafening blast of air in the cab.

Our highball signal consisted of two beeps on the air whistle. This was followed by loud blasts from the stacks of both locomotives as they worked to get our train rolling as quickly as possible. In the mountain terrain we always kept a sharp lookout for obstructions on the tracks, especially around curves and tunnels. If a train was blocking the

track ahead, torpedoes would signal the danger. One torpedo indicated stop; two warned a crew to proceed slowly. The detonation of torpedoes on the rails could easily be heard above the engine-cab noises. Another danger signal was a flare burning on the ties. A red flare meant stop, while a yellow one meant caution.

The biggest thrill of all, for me, was doubleheading a "Silk Train". At such times we would have a clear track right on through to Field. Leaving Golden with a "Silk Special", "Windy" McClean would yank the throttle wide open and leave it that way right up to Field. Those were the fastest and most hair-raising runs I ever made.

A typical "Silk Special" consisted of 7 or 8 express cars loaded with a million-dollar silk cargo from the Orient. The general idea was to get the cargo from ship-ports on the Pacific coast to eastern destinations - like New York - as quickly as possible. Due to its high insurance coverage, silk had rights over everything, even top passenger trains. At every stop, no matter how brief, guards would get out and patrol the train with submachine guns.

Of course, there was plenty of danger involved in mountain railroading. One time we entered a tunnel and I saw icicles hanging down inside. Even though my cab window was wide open, it was hot and I was thirsty. On a sudden impulse, I leaned far out and grabbed one of the icicles with my gloved left hand. I expected it simply to snap off, but it didn't budge. If I hadn't been gripping the window ledge with my right hand I could have been yanked off my feet and gone right out of the cab! Not a very pleasant idea. Although I quickly let go of the stubborn icicle, the sudden jolt had nearly dislocated my shoulder. When I signed off that trip I reported the injury to the time office, not giving any details, however. For a long time afterwards I was called only for trips on oil-burners!

As I think back to those fantastic times during the "Roaring Twenties", I believe there is no greater thrill on earth, for me, than riding in the cab of a steam locomotive, while thundering through those beautiful Canadian Rockies."

(Above) An eastbound train near Lake Louise is led by D-9 Class 4-6-0 No. 575 sometime around 1920, with Daly Glacier in the background.   Canadian Pacific Corporate Archives

In the Scenic Rockies

A Selection of Photographs by Nicholas Morant

(Above) During more than 50 years as Canadian Pacific's official photographer, Nick Morant recorded a wide variety of railway scenes, usually accompanied by his wife Willie, who is seen here waving to the crew of "Selkirk" No. 5904, with a freight train on Field Hill in the 1940s.
(Opposite) One of the first photos showing diesel power in the Canadian Rockies, with F7A No. 4062 leading the "Dominion" in 1952.   Both, Nicholas Morant Photos, from Canadian Pacific Corporate Archives

(Above) A double-headed "Troop Train" in the early 1940's is seen at the intermediate level of the Spiral Tunnels, led by 2-10-2 No. 5811 and 2-8-2 No. 5433.   Nicholas Morant/Canadian Pacific Corporate Archives

CANADIAN   PACIFIC

(Above) A 1940's double-headed freight train, eastbound at the Mount Stephen Tunnel and snowshed .
(Below) An 1950's eastbound passenger train after leaving the upper portal of the upper spiral tunnel.
Both, Nicholas Morant Photos, from Canadian Pacific Corporate Archives

(Above)
A westbound
freight headed
into the sunset
along the Bow
River in
August, 1951.

(Below) A
triple-headed
passenger train
working uphill
in the 1940's.
Both, Nicholas
Morant Photos/
Canadian Pacific
Corporate Archives

46

(Above) A westbound passenger train headed for Banff around 1950.

Nicholas Morant Photo/Canadian Pacific Corporate Archives

(Above) A mounted rider watches the westbound "Dominion" on its way into the Rockies near Canmore in 1948.

Nicholas Morant Photo/Canadian Pacific Corporate Archives

(Above) "The Mountaineer" along the Bow River, three miles east of Lake Louise in 1947. Nick Morant has taken so many classic photographs at this location that it has become known as "Morant's Curve."

Nicholas Morant Photo/Canadian Pacific Corporate Archives

(Above) "The Dominion" rolls through snow covered Banff National Park on its way west towards Banff, around 1950.

Photo by Nicholas Morant/Canadian Pacific Corporate Archives

(Above) Steam and smoke in the winter, as Selkirk No. 5927 races westbound with 13 cars along the Bow River.
(Below) A snowplow extra near Stephen, B.C. in January 1976.

Nicholas Morant Photos/Canadian Pacific Corporate Archives

(Above) The CPR's streamlined "Canadian" transcontinental passenger train is seen near Banff in the summer of 1955, led by No. 1417.

(Below) No. 4037 leads a 5-unit freight eastbound at Gap Lake in May 1955. This was towards the end of steam operations. Steamer in the middle of the train was headed for scrapping in Calgary.

(Opposite) A modern bulk train at the Great Divide - Summit of the Rockies.

Nicholas Morant Photos/Canadian Pacific Corporate Archives

(Above) A pair of "Mikes" and a caboose head back to Field after pusher duty on the hill. They are sister engines 5362 and 5363, seen on July 31, 1947.
(Below) Selkirk (2-10-4) No. 5925 is seen on the head of a passenger train at Yoho in June of 1951.

Both Photos, W.C. Whittaker

(Above) Only the most ambitious photographers got pictures of steam-powered trains at Yoho - especially if they had no car to reach this isolated mountain place, as in this case, with No. 5809 and a 5900 doubleheading a passenger train in 1951.

W.C. Whittaker Photo

Steam in the Rockies
As Seen Through the Lens of W.C. Whittaker

Inspired by pictures in magazines showing trains in the Canadian Rockies, Will Whittaker made two trips into the mountains by train, travelling up from his home in California. He was a photographer of railroads - a rail buff who went around in time to capture scenes of trains that most modern rail buffs can only dream about. Since he had no automobile with which to follow the trains, he spent several days on each of his trips to the Canadian Rockies hiking out along the tracks from various stations where he could lay over. In those days there were enough passenger trains daily that one could do a lot of laying over and commuting between Golden, Field, Banff, and Calgary.

Sometimes Will Whittaker went on his rail-photo excursions alone, other times with a fellow enthusiast. He recalls staying at many out-of-the-way towns where the only activity was railroad business. Back in those days cameras were not as common everywhere as they are today. There must have been more than one railroad-town citizen who wondered about this fellow travelling all the way from California just to take pictures of trains. He says: *"I'm sure thankful for the Chinese - they were always willing to cook up a meal and provide hospitality to a stranger. I was surprised to find them in so many of the small Canadian communities ... I'd be afraid to undertake those kind of (rail-photo) trips today, especially with the high price one must pay for accommodations."*

(Above) Santa Fe (2-10-2) No. 5810 and Selkirk (2-10-4) No. 5923 work their way uphill above Field with a passenger train on July 31, 1947.
(Below) One of the popular mountain-observation cars brings up the rear of this westbound passenger train heading down Field Hill in 1947.

W.C. Whittaker Photos

(Above) Selkirk No. 5906 leads a passenger train over the Kicking Horse River on July 30, 1947. The overhead gadget in front of the locomotive is called a tell-tale. It warned brakemen walking on top of freight cars that low clearance was coming up in the form of a bridge or tunnel entrance.

(Below) With tenders piled high from the coal chute at Field, a pair of Mikado 2-8-2's wheel their train of mixed freight along the Kicking Horse River in June 1951.　　　　Both Photos, W.C. Whittaker

(Above) Selkirk (2-10-4) No. 5926 rolls downhill into Field, leaving smoke, steam, dust, and heat in the wake of her passenger train on June 11, 1951.

(Below) A westbound passenger train behind No. 5906 follows the Kicking Horse River towards Golden in 1947.

(Above) Two of the C.P.R.'s Selkirk (2-10-4 type) locomotives were at the head of this passenger train as it wound its way through the Rockies along the Kicking Horse River on July 30, 1947, led by No. 5911.

(Below) Decapod (2-10-0 type) No. 5770 flies the white flags of an Extra Train as she runs light back down to Golden after helping to push a train up the Kicking Horse Pass on July 30, 1947. This class of locomotive was used mostly as mountain pushers out of Golden and Revelstoke. They were strong, but rough riding.

Both Photos, W.C. Whittaker

(Above) A show of power on Field Hill in the summer of 1947, this triple-header is led by 2-10-2 No. 5812 and a pair of Mikados.

(Below) At the other end of power ratings and in sharp contrast to the steady line of heavy trains and big locomotives was 1907-built D-10 class 4-6-0 No. 607, running extra with a spare tender and a string of flat cars. Engines like this were becoming rare in mainline service, especially on the mountains.

Both Photos, W.C. Whittaker

WESTWARD TRAINS—INFERIOR DIRECTION

LAGGAN SUBDIVISION

FOURTH CLASS		THIRD CLASS		SECOND CLASS	FIRST CLASS				Miles from Calgary	Telegraph and Telephone Offices	STATIONS	Telegraph Calls	Car Capacity Sidings	14
85	83	953	951	965	1	5	7	13						
Freight l Daily	Freight l Daily	Freight l Daily	Freight l Daily	Freight l Daily	Psgr. l Daily	Psgr. l Daily	Psgr. l Daily	Psgr. l Daily						Psg. a Da
—	—	—	—	—	12.40	8.40	7.35	6.45	.0	D N	CALGARY ZKX	C G	—	18.
											1.5			
13.30	24.05	18.45	9.00	22.15	12.55	8.45	7.50	7.00	1.5		SUNALTA			18.
											3.1			
13.35	24.10	18.50	9.05	22.20	13.00	8.51	7.57	7.07	4.6	P	BRICKBURN		84	17.
									8.7		ROBERTSON		Nil	
											0.9			
13.44	24.18	18.58	9.13	22.28	13.07	8.58	8.05	7.15	9.6	P	KEITH	Z	88	17.
											4.6			
13.53	24.26	19.06	9.21	22.36	13.14	9.04	8.12	7.22	14.2	P	BEARSPAW		86	17.
											3.7			
14.01	24.33	19.13	9.28	22.42	13.20	9.10	8.18	7.29	17.9	P	GLENBOW		86	17.
											4.9			
14.10	24.41	19.21	9.36	22.50	13.27	s 9.19	f 8.26	7.37	22.8	D	COCHRANE	Z U N	84	17.
											5.0			
14.19	24.50	19.36	9.44	22.58	13.34	9.26	8.34	7.44	27.8	D	MITFORD	Z M F	68	17.
											6.0			
14.30	1.00	19.50	9.54	23.07	13.42	9.35	8.43	7.53	33.8	P	RADNOR		87	17.
											3.8			
14.38	1.07	19.57	10.01	23.13	13.47	9.40	8.49	7.59	37.6	P	CHENEKA		55	17.
											4.0			
14.46	1.15	20.04	10.08	23.20	13.53	s 9.46	8.58	8.08	41.6	D N	MORLEY	Z Z	88	17.
											5.9			
15.05	1.30	20.21	10.22	23.35	14.00	9.54	9.06	8.16	47.5	P	OZADA		84	16.
											4.6			
15.15	1.40	20.30	10.30	23.45	14.06	s 10.01	9.13	8.23	52.1	P	SEEBE	Z	110	16.
											2.2			
15.20	1.45	20.34	10.35	23.49	14.09	10.05	9.17	8.27	54.3	P	KANANASKIS		Nil	16.
											3.0			
15.25	1.50	20.39	10.40	23.54	14.13	s 10.13	f 9.25	8.35	57.3	D	EXSHAW	Z S F	80	16.
											5.4			
15.35	1.59	20.48	10.58	24.03	14.20	10.20	9.33	8.43	62.7	P	GAP		85	16.
											4.4			
15.55	2.07	20.56	11.06	24.10	14.27	s 10.32	f 9.44	8.52	67.1	D N	CANMORE	Y D	179	16.
											4.9			
16.14	2.15	21.04	11.14	24.18	14.33	10.40	9.52	9.01	72.0	P	DUTHIL		85	16.
											5.2			
16.25	2.24	21.12	11.23	24.27	14.40	10.48	10.00	9.10	77.2		ANTHRACITE		Nil	16.
											4.7			
16.40	2.35	21.20	11.31	24.35	s 14.50 / 14.55	s 10.55 / 11.05	s 10.10 / 10.20	s 9.20 / 9.40	81.9	D N	V BANFF VZYW	B F	273	1-2 s 16. / s 14.
											6.2			
16.50	2.45	21.35	11.40	24.45	15.05	11.15	10.30	9.50	88.1	P	SAWBACK		86	14.
											4.9			
17.00	3.06	21.45	11.48	24.55	15.15	11.22	10.38	9.58	93.0	P	MASSIVE		85	14.
											6.0			
17.10	3.16	21.55	11.58	1.05	15.25	11.30	10.47	10.07	99.0	P	CASTLE MOUNTAIN		86	14.
											7.7			
17.31	3.40	22.07	12.10	1.17	15.35	11.40	10.58	10.18	106.7	P	ELDON		86	14.
											4.0			
17.40	3.50	22.15	12.16	1.24	15.40	11.45	11.04	10.24	110.7	P	TEMPLE		85	14.
											5.9			
18.25	4.00	22.25	12.25	1.35	s 15.55	s 12.00	s 11.20	s 10.35 / 10.45	116.6	D N	V LAKE LOUISE VZYW	R	91 / 48	14. / s 13.
											5.6			
18.50	4.20	22.45	12.45	1.55	16.10	12.15	11.35	11.00	122.2	P	STEPHEN	Z	85	14.
											2.8			
19.00	4.30	22.55	12.55	2.04	16.17	12.22	11.42	11.07	125.0	P	HECTOR	Z	41	13.
											2.8			
19.10	4.40	23.05	13.05	2.13	16.25	12.30	11.50	11.15	127.8		PARTRIDGE		Nil	13
											2.0			
19.20	4.50	23.15	13.20	2.21	16.35	12.37	11.57	11.22	129.8	P	YOHO	Z	86	13.
											2.6			
19.30	5.00	23.25	13.30	2.30	16.45	12.45	12.05	11.30	132.4	P	CATHEDRAL		86	13
											4.2			
19.45	5.15	23.40	13.45	2.45	17.00	13.00	12.20	11.45	136.6	D N	V FIELD ZK	A C	l 13. / a 12	
a Daily 85	a Daily 83	a Daily 953	a Daily 951	a Daily 965	a Daily 1	a Daily 5	a Daily 7	a Daily 13		Rule 93a applies between Sunalta and Field				l Da 14

Double Track (Calgary Terminals) · Automatic Block Signal System

SEE LAGGAN SUBDIVISION FOOT NOTES AND SPECIAL

(Above) Milk cans await the next mixed train going southward from Golden on this summer day in 1947, a time when several passenger trains still stopped here daily. The handsome 1904 station remained in service from steamboat days until almost the end of passenger trains to Golden and is now preserved for historical purposes.

W.C. Whittaker Photo

• GOLDEN •

"The train suddenly emerges into daylight as Golden is reached. The broad river ahead is the Columbia moving northward. The supremely beautiful mountains beyond are the Selkirks, rising from their forest-clad bases and lifting their ice-crowned heads far into the sky. They extend in an apparently unbroken line from the southwest to the northeast, gradually melting into the remote distance. They are matchless in form, and when bathed in the light of the afternoon sun, their radiant warmth and glory of color suggest Asgard, the celestial city of Scandinavian story. Parallel with them and rising eastward from the Columbia, range upon range, are the Rockies, only the loftiest peaks to be seen just now over the massive benches upon which they rest.

Golden is a mining town upon the bank of the Columbia, at the mouth of the Wapta (Kicking Horse). During the summer months, a steamer makes weekly trips from here up the Columbia to the lakes at the head of the river, 100 miles distant and this is the point of departure for the famous East Kootenay mining district. About Golden, and at various places above, especially at the base of the Spillimichene Mts., gold and silver mines are being developed. From the head of navigation, roads and trails lead over to the Findlay Creek mining district and to the Kootenay Valley. The trip up the river is a most desirable one for sportsmen. From Golden to Donald, the railway follows down the Columbia on the face of the lower bench of the Rocky Mts., the Selkirks all the way in full view opposite, the soft green streaks down their sides indicating the paths of avalanches..."

From a C.P.R. Tour Guide of the 1880's

(Above) The painters are hard at work on Golden's two-stall engine house in this 1916 scene. Note the water barrels on the roof and the ancient boxcar on the left.

(Below) Ten-Wheeler No. 581 awaits a trip south on the Kootenay Central mixed train in this 1947 view, which also shows mainline pusher No. 5770, plus Golden's engine servicing plant, including (from right): Fuel oil tank, sand tower, enclosed water tower and water standpipe.

W.C. Whittaker Photo

(Below Right) By 1971 Golden saw only one passenger train daily in each direction, and that ended altogether with the government cuts of 1990.

AHW Photo

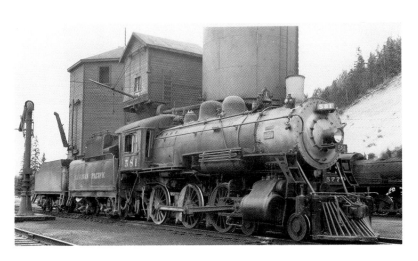

S. 15." GOLDEN GREETS GOLDEN JUBILEE TRAIN.

(Above) This special train was pulled into Golden by No. 5905, one of the original twenty "Selkirk" type (2-10-4) locomotives built by Montreal Locomotive Works. Information with the picture calls this the "Golden Jubilee Train of 1925," but Golden didn't have a jubilee in that year, and the first Selkirks weren't built until 1929. This was the largest engine in the British Empire at the time, weighing 750,000 lbs. in working order. No. 5905 spent most of her working life in the Rockies and Selkirks, which is how her class got the name.

Photo by Byron Harmon/Archives of Canadian Rockies

(Below) Looking back towards the town of Golden from the caboose of a passing westbound freight, we see D-10 class 4-6-0 No. 911 making up its mixed train for the return trip to Cranbrook. By the time of this September 1952 photo, the mainline itself was mostly dieselized.

Rail Photo Service/AHW Collection

(Above) Selkirk No. 5911 picks up speed quickly as she hauls an Eastbound Express Train out of Golden on July 29, 1947. The interesting short consist includes a vintage flat-roofed wooden express car with truss rods (mid-train), and a wooden caboose for the trainmen. This engine was involved in a rather freak accident one winter when it was hit by a snow slide. The impact tore off the tender, which rolled back downgrade by itself and almost silently slaughtered a crew of track workers shoveling snow.
W.C. Whittaker Photo

(Below) The first diesel-powered train came into Golden in January of 1949, while winter was going strong. Three demonstrator units were eastbound in the mountainous steam country with a special passenger train, when this photo was taken during a stop-over by the water tank. The units were painted and lettered for General Motors Diesel Ltd. By the end of 1952 all passenger trains through Golden were hauled by diesels, except the Kootenay Central Mixed.
John Poulsen Photo

The Kootenay Central Railway

"The Kootenay Central R.R. in course of construction now makes it possible to place upon the market the fruit lands of this Happy Valley in Southern British Columbia, consisting of the Windermere and Wilmer districts. This valley, known as the Columbia River Valley or Windermere Valley, lies between two great western systems of the Canadian Pacific Railway, the main line on the north and the Crow's Nest Pass branch to the south and has on the east the Rocky Mountains and on the west the rugged Selkirks. This is the last, and undoubtedly the richest, undeveloped part of this river's wonderful valley".

1911 Advertisement

The Kootenay Central Railway Company was incorporated in 1901 to build a line from the Crow's Nest branch of the C.P.R. at Wardner, to Fort Steele, Canal Flats, Lake Windermere, and Golden on the transcontinental mainline. However, there was no pressing reason for constructing such a rail line. For the next few years it was never certain that the line would be built, at all. And for nearly fifty years after it was built there was only light traffic. Today, however, the Kootenay Central is the busiest branch line on C.P. Rail's system.

Less than twenty years before the Kootenay Central's incorporation the valley through which it was built remained largely wild and uninhabited. The main settlements were tipi camps of the nomadic Kootenay Indians, who roamed from north of Golden down into Montana and Idaho. In addition, there were some miners and a few ranchers. Riverboats hauled on water whatever traffic couldn't be handled by horses and wagons over the old Indian trails that had been crudely widened.

In 1903 the Kootenay Central Railway received its first cash subsidy from the Federal Government to help with construction. President and chief guiding force of the line was C. Hungerford Pollen, who made his office in Cranbrook. The C.P.R. was the financial backer from the start, although there was talk of the Great Northern extending its branch in British Columbia as far north as Golden.

The September 1, 1904 issue of The Outcrop, from Wilmer, B.C., carried the following news of the K.C.'s progress:

Kootenay Central Ry.

"The surveyors working from the Golden end of the Kootenay Central Railway were camped 27 miles from that town on Monday, and the men at the other end were about 34 miles from Crow's Nest and about four miles from Fort Steele ... A late arrival from Steele states that he did not see any grading stakes along the portion he saw surveyed and

thinks the rumor false. The Prospector says that from the most reliable source it learns that construction will commence this fall and be completed in 1905. The latest C.P.R. maps have this railway marked as already completed".

After the initial survey was completed, the C.P.R. continued to debate the matter of building a railroad up this valley. Several representatives were sent out to inspect the area for future traffic potential. All agreed that the railroad line could operate profitably, but company men in the east were still not convinced. By 1907 only 15 miles of rail had been laid southward, along the Columbia River, from Golden. For some time this was the extent of the proposed K.C. Railway, as the following letter shows. It was written on December 26th, 1908 by C.P.R. Second Vice President Whyte, to his assistant, J.S. Dennis:

"With reference to your letter of the 14th in respect to the KC Ry. If the steel were laid over the 15 miles at the north end we might have to put it into operation, and what traffic would we derive from it? Would not as much be served by team?

"For the present the bridge which the Columbia Lumber Company have over the Kicking Horse should be sufficient to enable us to lay track. While it will not carry one of our larger engines yet I understand that the Co. operate a smaller engine over the bridge, and that all traffic at the present time is being teamed into Golden.

We are doing sufficient work on this branch now to fulfill the conditions of the charter and I would have great hesitation in doing anything further just now unless it is considered the amount of additional traffic we would derive would warrant it or unless we could collect the subsidy on the fifteen miles".

One reason the Kootenay Central line was slow in being built was that the builders could not decide which of several proposed routes to follow. Of particular concern was the southern terminus of the line - where should it connect to the Crow's Nest line, which was already in operation? The original charter called for the tracks to run from Colvalli to Golden via Fort Steele. However, the citizens of Cranbrook felt that *their* town would make a more logical junction point. The Cranbrook Board of Trade went so far as to hire a former C.P.R. survey engineer named Parker to conduct barometric readings which would prove that a line directly to Cranbrook would be most efficient. C.P.R. records show the following correspondence on the matter, written by the assistant to the second vice president.

A Tourist Map published around 1913.
Glenbow-Alberta Institute

67

"...The route proposed by Mr. Parker (to Cranbrook) entirely side tracks Fort Steele and is, therefore, such a departure from the route covered by the K.C. charter that an amendment of that charter would be required before anything could be done ... and personally it would seem to me that the proposal put up by the Cranbrook Board of Trade is a very weak one".

The second vice president replied to his assistant on August 27, 1909, by saying:

"...If we consider at this late date the proposition made by the people of Cranbrook, it would only delay the completion of the line, and ...would require the amending of the charter. Further, we are getting a much easier grade at a comparatively low cost for construction, by leaving the Crow's Nest line east of the Kootenay River, than we can get by leaving the branch west of the Kootenay...to run into Cranbrook..."

In fact, by the following spring, C.P.R. officials were questioning whether the Kootenay Central's construction should be continued, at all. The man most concerned was Hungerford Pollen, president of the K.C. Railway, who had spent a number of years promoting the project. The following letter was written by J.S.. Dennis, assistant to the second vice president, to his immediate superior, W. Whyte, whose office was in Winnipeg. The letter is dated April 16, 1909, and marked "Personal".

"Dear Sir, - Some days ago Mr. Pollen called upon me and referred to the interviews he had with the President (of the C.P.R.) and yourself relative to the construction of the Kootenay Central.
"I gathered from what Mr. Pollen said that the President and yourself were expecting a further report from me regarding the possibilities of traffic on this line and I told Mr. Pollen that though I thought you already had my views on this point I would write again dealing with the matter as fully as possible.
As I see it, the position regarding the Kootenay Central stands as follows.
We have a contract with that Company under which we share with them the subsidy earned by construction of the line or pay them so much a mile if we do not build the line.
The facts for and against the construction of the line may be summarized as under.

Against The Construction
(a) The statement of the Engineering Department that it would be an exceptionally expensive line to construct and operate.

(b) The statement of the Engineering Department that sufficient traffic cannot be developed in the Columbia and Kootenay Valleys to justify construction.

For The Construction
(1) The actual location surveys for the line have proved that there are no exceptional engineering difficulties to be overcome and have provided approximate estimates of the cost of the construction.
(2) The fact that the construction of the line will earn a subsidy which after paying the share due to owners of the charter will leave a considerable amount to apply on cost of construction.
(3) The information obtained by your own trip through the Columbia Valley, as to its possibilities in the way of settlement and development.
(4) The information contained in my reports after two trips through the Valley that it contains as much or more land available and suitable for agriculture and horticulture than all the other Valleys of the Kootenay region.
(5) The report of Mr. Macdonald, Ass't General Freight Agent, after a trip through the Valley, that the traffic possibilities were encouraging.
(6) The reports of Professor Lake, Mr. Palmer and Mr. Sharpe of Aggasiz Experimental Farm that the Valley is well suited for growth of fruit and that for growth of apples the Valley is probably better than the other Valleys of Southern British Columbia.
(7) The very full report of Mr. W. Pearce, Ass't British Columbia Land Commissioner, as to the suitability of the Valley for settlement.
(8) The fact that after careful personal inspection of conditions, Messrs. Bruce, Beisecker & Davidson have undertaken the completion of an irrigation system about midway in the Valley which will render ten thousand acres of land available for agriculture and horticulture.
(9) The fact that twenty thousand tons of ore are blocked out in the Paradise Mine at Wilmer, which will be shipped as soon as line is completed, and that while there are no other large developed mines in the Valley there are many promising prospects which will be developed and proved as soon as there is railway communication.
(10) The certainty that a large immediate traffic in lumber and ties would develop, especially along the Southerly half of the line, the moment it is finished.
(11) The fact now admitted by everyone who has been through the Valley, that the construction of the line would provide in the vicinity of Windermere Lakes, a "Tourist playground" with facilities and attractions not available at any of the present resorts on existing lines in the mountains.
(12) The fact that construction of the line through the Columbia Valley would afford a route for shipment of grain from extreme southern portion of Alberta to Vancouver and return traffic with low grades as compared with even revised grades on west slope of the Rocky Mountains.
(13) The final fact that the Columbia and Kootenay Valleys are "wide open" for the construction of a low grade branch of the Crows Nest Southern Railway (Great Northern) which would direct traffic to the South (into the U.S.A.)..."

The last statement made in this letter probably had more to do with the company's final decision to go ahead and build the Kootenay Central than any other. The C.P.R. was then waging a battle for control of Canadian rail operations along the international boundary with the American-owned Great Northern. If the Great Northern had built the Kootenay Central line instead of the C.P.R., much lumber and mining traffic would have gone from Canada directly down into the States.

The government land grant for fulfilling the original charter of the British Columbia Southern Railway totaled close to half a million acres. Included were 13,392 acres of agricultural land, 37,260 acres of grazing land, and most of the rest valuable at least for its timber. A lot of this land was along the Kootenay Central line, making an important factor in the prospective settling of future railroad customers.

In the fall of 1909 the C.P.R. took one more look at their involvement with the Kootenay Central, of which only a few miles were yet in operation. On November 2 of that year, W. Whyte sent the following coded telegram to his assistant, J.S. Dennis in Calgary: (Actual meaning in parentheses).

"Escaping (engineer) Wilkin left here today for Cull Cable (Cranbrook) to run reconnaissance of possible loser (line) from touted (there) for drunkard (decision) of kootenay Cherub (Central) as suggested by Proficiency (President) when west. Please arrange for some member your department meet and accompany him to make report on quality and character of lecturer (country) enroute. Please wire who it will be."

President Pollen of the Kootenay Central, in his Cranbrook office, was getting concerned over the lack of action because his charter was running out. With the American-owned Great Northern casting eyes in the direction of the Kootenay Central line, Hungerford risked losing out on the dividends promised by the C.P.R. for taking over his charter. He put all his efforts into persuading the C.P.R. to build the line, and the provincial government into subsidizing that building. He also got Cranbrook's help with his provincial negotiations by offering that *"the route will be more carefully weighed in their interests, and that they will have a right to demand consideration which at present neither this town nor this province are entitled to."*

From the C.P.R. he asked, *"Could you therefore get me an assurance that the road will be constructed and that all consideration will be given to the people here, if the subsidy is revived".* After a business trip west, the C.P.R.'s President, Sir Thomas Shaughnessy, made the final decision in early 1910 to go ahead with the Kootenay Central Railway as a branch. The decision was, of course, applauded by all those who lived in the area and wanted to see it developed. The **Rossland Miner** of April 6, 1910, carried the following story:

C.P.R. Kind to Kootenay
Construction of Branch from Elko
on Crow's Nest Arouses Interest

"The news that the C.P.R. will commence construction of the Kootenay Central Railway this spring is hailed with delight by the people in the valley of the Kootenay who have been looking for many years for this proposed road.

The road, when completed, will extend from Elko on the Crow's Nest branch to Golden on the main line, and will follow the Kootenay River ...

Fort Steele is a beautiful location for a town. The site is large, level and covered with magnificent bull pines. It is surrounded on three sides by the Kootenay River and the valley of the Wild Horse. The fourth side extends in rolling foothills up to the rocky Steeple ranges, which are rich in gold and iron ...

The railroad will ... revive old Fort Steele, as iron mining will then be pushed forward."

But apparently there was still a great deal of uncertainty among the people of the Valley as to when and where the rail line would be built. The matter was discussed in an exchange of letters between the C.P.R.'s J.S. Dennis, in Calgary, and H.G. Parson, a pioneer settler of Golden, as well as its M.L.A. to the Provincial Legislature in Victoria. Parson wrote on May 4th, saying:

"Dear Mr. Dennis, Without wishing to be too inquisitive, I should like very much to know if it is intended to go ahead this summer with the Model Swiss Village here. I should also be glad to know if you would be willing to use your influence to have the names "Golden" and "Windermere" given to new standard sleeping cars as soon as practicable, as well as "Mount Moberly" to an observation car when the opportunity offers. I will not bother you with anything else just now, not even the "K.C.R." Yours truly H.G. Parson."

The reply from J.S. Dennis is dated May 9th, 1910. The Swiss Village herein being referred to was to house a number of mountain guides that the C.P.R. had brought over from Switzerland to settle in the Canadian Rockies. The guides served the railway for surveying and reconnaissance, as well as for tourist parties and general publicity.

"Dear Mr. Parsons: - I have your letter of the 4th instant. Replying to your question regarding the Swiss Village, I beg to say that we are now having a design for the subdivision of the land prepared, and it is our intention to go on at once with this subdivision and the construction of the first six typical Swiss cottages. I hope that we will be able to get this work well under way in the very near future.

Referring to your request regarding names for sleepers and one of the observation cars. I have today written the Vice President at Montreal, asking him to meet your wishes in this matter, if possible.

I understood that Mr. Bruce informed you, during his late visit to Golden, that the matter of the construction of the Kootenay Central, might be looked upon as settled finally, and I am in hopes that very shortly the work will be well under way and progressing vigorously. Yours truly, J.S. Dennis."

Actual work still did not go ahead very fast. More than two years passed before passenger trains from the Crow's Nest could even go as far as Fort Steele, which is today the junction point for the start of the Kootenay Central branch. **The Cranbrook Prospector** of October 5, 1912 ran the following story:

"Tuesday, Oct. 1st, was a Red Letter day for the residents of Fort Steele, the occasion being the arrival of the first regular passenger train over the Kootenay Central Railway from Fernie and other towns in the Crow's Nest Pass. A large number of people from Fernie visited the pioneer city of the Kootenay.

A regular daily train service is now established between Cranbrook, Fernie and other towns in the pass. Trains will leave Fernie at 7 a.m. for Fort Steele, connecting at Elko with the Local that leaves Cranbrook at 7 a.m., returning at 7 p.m. Distance from Fernie to Fort Steele by the new route is 61 miles, and about the same from Cranbrook to Fort Steele via the railroad."

The decision had been made to connect the Kootenay Central with the Crows Nest branch at Colvalli, east of Cranbrook and Fort Steele, instead of running the line directly into Cranbrook, as it does today. Because of this indirect connection, passenger service between Cranbrook and Golden was never very popular. For many years a stage service was operated to haul mail and passengers between Cranbrook and Fort Steele, making a connection with the north and southbound trains. The stage required a ride of ten or eleven miles, as against the train's total of 60 miles via Wardner, Colvalli and Bull River. In later years a motor stage replaced the one drawn by horses.

In the **Golden Star** of March 15, 1913 was this news:
"Final contracts let on Kootenay Central Railway. Three and a half million dollars worth of work to be carried out by Spokane Contractors. Burns & Jordan to build final 60 miles of the Jukeson to Golden cutoff in the Windermere Valley. They will employ about 2,000 men, and will keep 5 or 6 steam shovels at work. They will have about 20 camps, and expect to take about 2 years to do the work."
In November of 1913 the news was:
"Will Lay Track to Spillimachene. "Rails should enter that place early next month ... Twenty cars of steel, sufficient for about seven miles of track, are now on hand, and a track laying machine will arrive here in a day or so from Winnipeg having been billed out of there by red card freight some days ago."

During 1913 steamboats still did a lot of the transporting work up and down the Columbia and Kootenay Rivers, especially during the summer months when there was much tourist traffic. Some motor-powered boats were also put in service. In fact, the last of the sternwheelers in the East Kootenays was built in 1913, ironically to help with the railroad construction which would bring an end to the boat business.

This last boat was the F.P. ARMSTRONG, built by a noted riverboat captain of the same name, at Spillimachene. She worked for contractors Burns & Jordan during the next two years. The contractors also used their own dinky locomotive and dump cars to build the rail line. When the work was finished, the F.P. ARMSTRONG was abandoned near Fairmont Hot Springs.

The Superintendent of Railway Mail Service made preparations in 1913 for his department to take over mail delivery from the steamboats. In a letter to the Columbia Valley Irrigation Company he said:

"...I also noticed in the same paper that a steamer had been constructed to run between Spilmachene and Invermere. I understand your mail service at present is two trips per week by steamer and one by stage from Golden. Would you consider it would be of more advantage to the people of the Columbia Valley to have mail by the railway to Spilmachene three times per week and from that point to have the steamer take it to the different villages or to leave the service as it is for the summer and make new arrangements in the fall?..."

By January, 1914, the **Golden Star** reported that the northern part of the Kootenay Central was within 20 miles of Athalmer. The same issue mentioned the interesting fact that *"throughout one of the winters of the early 90's there was absolutely no snow in Golden."*

As the railroad approached the Lake Windermere area local residents had a controversy over the future station's name. Athalmer was the only community directly on the line. On the hill, above, was Invermere, which had originally been named Canterbury by its early settlers who came from Britain. A little further away, across the lake, was the town of Windermere, with a band of Kootenay Indians on an adjacent reserve. All these groups were to be served by one C.P.R. station, and few wanted it named Athalmer. On August 8th, 1914 it was announced that the station would be officially designated as Lake Windermere, and that *"the very nature of it carries a note of surpassing beauty to all persons familiar with the famous Windermere District of England..."*

Work on the railway was rushed with all speed as the winter of 1914 approached. All major grading and track laying had to be completed before heavy frosts got into the soft earth, which was expected to be during December. Finally came the long-awaited announcement in local papers, such as this one, in the **Golden Star:**

"Working on the Railroad"
Scenes of Building the Kootenay Central near Invermere, B.C. in 1914. Shown are steam shovels, cars, a locomotive, and a huge track laying machine.

John Poulsen Collection

"Last Spike Driven in Kootenay Central"

"The last spike connecting the steel on the Kootenay Central Railway was driven on Thursday afternoon, December 3 (1914), at 3 o'clock. This ceremony was performed a few miles south of Athalmer and was witnessed by a number of officials of the company and prominent residents of the district.

During the last ten days Windermere Lake was covered with its first sheet of ice for the season. This closing down of the year marks the finish of river navigation on the Columbia for freight and passengers and when next the question of transportation arises the traffic will be by rail. It is now a little over 107 years since David Thompson, an explorer and as-

tronomer for the North West Company of Montreal, launched his canoe on the Columbia at a point north of the mainline of the C.P.R...."

On December 11, 1914 the news read: *"First through passenger train over the Kootenay Central got into Golden last night at 5:15, in charge of Conductor Shackleton, with Engineer Atchison at the throttle."*

On January 1, 1915 another report said: *"The first scheduled or regular train pulled into Lake Windermere Station. It was a cold, bleak morning; a fog steamed up from the Columbia River. Gus Erickson, Divisional Superintendent from Cranbrook, was in command. A few soldiers were aboard, enroute to the World's First Great War."*

(Above) Along the Kootenay Central in 1914 was this fine railway station, sitting on the banks of the Columbia River. The sign-painter had his own way of spelling Spillimacheen, although the C.P.R. has spelled it different.

(Below) The same station looking north, with a horse and several automobiles awaiting the arrival of a train.   Both photos/Canadian Pacific Corporate Archives

For the next fifty years the Kootenay Central line was just another branch in the Canadian Pacific Railway's far-flung operations. The Valley never developed to the point that optimists had predicted. Neither fruit farming nor grain growing became very important, and there were not many mines or lumber mills operated at any one time. Much of the traffic over the line was being interchanged from the mainline at Golden to the secondary mainline through the Crow's Nest. Several times during the Forties and Fifties there were rumors that the C.P.R. was going to abandon the Kootenay Central altogether.

For most of its history, passenger service on the Kootenay Central was by mixed train, usually with a coach and a combine attached to the rear of the freight cars. Steam power was originally one of the C.P.R.'s light 4-6-0's of the 400-class, with 2-8-0's being used occasionally. In later years the mixed train was generally hauled by one of the railroad's D-10's that were so popular for branch line service. Number 581 was a regular on the train for many years. When diesels replaced steam on the Kootenay Central, late in 1953 and early in 1954, the mixed train was usually hauled by a GP7. Shortly after 1960 the service was dropped altogether. Highways had made travel by train outmoded in the valley. The seats were mostly empty, and even express goods were sent by truck instead of train. Finally the post office changed its mailing to trucks, so the combine was no longer needed on trains.

(Upper Right) A typical southbound mixed train of the 1930's, near Parson, behind a vintage 2-8-0.

John Poulsen Collection

(Lower Right) Northbound Mixed stopped at Parson about 1922. Note the aged baggage car lettered Dominion-Atlantic, a long ways from home.

Hazel Cuffling Collection

(Below) The Kootenay Central Mixed leaving Golden in 1947, trailing Caboose No. 436732. Note the odd-looking bridge over the Kicking Horse River. Designed wrong, it wouldn't fit as planned, so the angle support beams on the right were left off. Only one was used from each truss, instead of both.

W.C. Whittaker Photo

CANADIAN
PACIFIC
RAILWAY

LAKE
WINDERMERE
CAMP

In the
Canadian Pacific Rockies

(Above) A northbound mixed train pulls up to Lake Windermere station behind No. 581 on this summer day in 1947. The coach of the train is out of view on the left, behind 40 freight cars. In back is the road uphill to Invermere, where the old log station now rests as a museum.   W.C. Whittaker Photo

NORTHWARD TRAINS INFERIOR DIRECTION		Miles from Fort Steele	Yard Limits	WINDERMERE SUBDIVISION STATIONS	Train Order Office Signals	Car Capacity Sidings	Siding Capacity in feet	SOUTHWARD TRAINS SUPERIOR DIRECTION				
								Fourth Class				
								80 Freight Daily	82 Freight Daily	84 Freight Daily	86 Freight Daily	
. . . . . .	. . . . . .	0.0	↑ 3.6	FORT STEELE . . . . RYZ Jct. Cranbrook Sub.	FS	Yard		0600		1400	2200	. . . . . .
			12.0									
. . . . . .	. . . . . .	12.0		WASA		154	8517	0539		1339	2139	. . . . . .
			20.4 10.3									
. . . . . .	. . . . . .	22.3	20.4 23.8 }	SKOOKUMCHUCK RWYZ	SK	51	2782	0520	0850	1320	2120	. . . . . .
			6.2									
. . . . . .	. . . . . .	28.5		TORRENT		Nil		0508	0838	1308	2108	. . . . . .
			11.0									
. . . . . .	. . . . . .	39.5	37.1 42.1 }	CANAL FLATS . . . . YZ		170	9364	0448	0818	1248	2048	. . . . . .
			5.5									
. . . . . .	. . . . . .	45.0		COLUMBIA LAKE		Nil		0438	0808	1238	2038	. . . . . .
			8.7									
. . . . . .	. . . . . .	53.7		FAIRMONT		172	9481	0420	0750	1220	2020	. . . . . .
			15.1									
. . . . . .	. . . . . .	68.8	66.0 71.1 }	WINDERMERE . . . . WYZ	AR	144	7928	0348	0718	1148	1948	. . . . . .
			8.8									
. . . . . .	. . . . . .	77.6	77.0 78.4 }	RADIUM . . . . Z		Nil		0330	0700	1130	1930	. . . . . .
			5.4									
. . . . . .	. . . . . .	83.0		EDGEWATER		Nil		0320	0650	1120	1920	. . . . . .
			5.0									
. . . . . .	. . . . . .	88.0		LUXOR		152	8374	0310	0640	1110	1910	. . . . . .
			6.0									
. . . . . .	. . . . . .	94.0	93.0 94.7 }	BRISCO . . . . Z		Nil		0258	0628	1058	1858	. . . . . .
			7.6									
. . . . . .	. . . . . .	101.6	100.0 104.3 }	SPILLIMACHEEN . . . Z	MA	151	8313	0245	0615	1045	1845	. . . . . .
			7.0									
. . . . . .	. . . . . .	108.6		HARROGATE		Nil		0233	0603	1033	1833	. . . . . .
			9.1									
. . . . . .	. . . . . .	117.7	116.5	SEENEY		155	8532	0216	0546	1016	1816	. . . . . .
			1.9									
. . . . . .	. . . . . .	119.6	↓ 120.3	PARSON . . . . Z		Nil		0213	0543	1013	1813	. . . . . .
			7.4									
. . . . . .	. . . . . .	127.0		McMURDO		Nil		0200	0530	1000	1800	. . . . . .
			7.0									
. . . . . .	. . . . . .	134.0		HORSE CREEK		152	8375	0148	0518	0948	1748	. . . . . .
			4.0									
. . . . . .	. . . . . .	138.0		NICHOLSON		Nil		0140	0510	0940	1740	. . . . . .
			4.5									
. . . . . .	. . . . . .	142.5	138.7 ↑	GOLDEN . . . . . . KZ Jct. Mountain Sub.	GD	Yard		0130	0500	0930	1730	. . . . . .

75

(Above) Built in 1923, this beautiful log station replaced an earlier one that was little more than a tiny shed, with two retired boxcars attached for freight storage. This scene is on July 29, 1947.

W.C. Whittaker Photo

Near Disaster at Lake Windermere Station

It was almost twenty minutes to seven in the morning of the last Monday of September, 1975. The weather was cool and clear; Lake Windermere lay still, recovering from the busy days of summer just past. People in Invermere and Athalmer were waking up to head for work and school. Many of them felt the deep rumbling of the earth as the familiar sound of a heavy freight train began to fill the air. It was headed up the valley with 105 cars of coal from Crow's Nest Pass.

In the old log station marked Lake Windermere, Mrs. Georgina Connell was the operator. As the train approached the station she went out the front door with two train order hoops to pass to the crews. The highway crossing signal rang loudly, as

the red lights flashed through the early morning mist. Locomotive headlights beamed ahead and reflected off the tops of the shiny rails, making them look like two long, slithering snakes. The diesel horns blasted through the air to warn motorists of the unstoppable stream of might that was about to cut through the roadway. The operator stood with her feet apart, facing the approaching train. Her left arm was held stiff and slightly bent, while the left hand held the wooden hoop. In a moment the massive locomotives rumbled by and an engineer's jacketed arm reached out and went through the hoop. With deft fingers the engineer removed the rolled up papers that were his train orders, and then flung the empty hoop back out to the side of the track.

Nearby, a yellow school bus had come to a stop at the crossing, a short distance from the flashing red lights and the heavy train that they warned of. Driver of the bus was Alfred Tegart, member of a large family of local pioneers. Alfred had watched trains at this crossing all his life. He was on his way to pick up high school students going to Invermere.

Suddenly something made Alfred Tegart feel strange about the moving train. On a hunch, he put his bus in reverse and moved away from the tracks. Sparks were shooting out from under some of the loaded cars, and then a rail broke. Tegart immediately flashed his bus lights on and off and began yelling from his opened window towards the station.

Operator Connell realized that something was going wrong, as she stood and waited to pass the other order hoop to the conductor on the caboose. She ducked down and saw the broken rail and realized the immense danger that was likely to explode at any moment. She ran into the station and pushed the button on her radio-phone so she could scream to the engineer: "Broken rail!" Then she continued on up the small stairs at the rear of the building.

The alerted engineer applied all his brakes in the emergen-

cy position, but the derailed cars were already in the process of turning over and being stopped the hard way. Some of them smashed through the front of the station and one totaled Mrs. Connell's car which was parked at one end. Alfred Tegart watched horrified and helpless, thinking that the train would soon smash the whole station to pieces. He didn't expect to see the operator alive again. When the train finally stopped, he ran down to the station, grabbed a plank, and broke a window at the back. He found the operator still on the stairs, in shock, so he helped her out through the window and took her to the hospital in his school bus. She was treated for shock and cuts and was released later that day.

Cleanup of the wreck took several days. Railroad officials declared the station useless and ordered a replacement. In a short time a green and white mobile home was set up just north of the damaged station, and soon the Lake Windermere sign hung from its side. Later, the old station was donated by CP Rail to the Windermere Valley Historical Society. This group moved the building to the top of the hill overlooking the tracks and station site. There it was carefully rebuilt and turned into the main building of a small Valley museum complex.

(Below) Two views of Lake Windermere's handsome log station not long before a coal train ran into it. Trucks later moved it uphill on the road behind, where it is now part of a museum.   Both, AHW Photos

(Above) Sunset on the Kootenay Central line near Radium Hot Springs in the 1970's with a unit coal-train headed for the Pacific Coast.
Nicholas Morant Photo/Canadian Pacific Corporate Archives

(Opposite, Top) A southbound "Plow Extra" clears the Kootenay Central line two miles north of Parson, after a heavy snow storm on December 12, 1977. The photo shows why engineers call this "blind flying."
W.R. Hooper Photo

(Opposite Bottom) A northbound freight trailing caboose No. 436676 skirts the shores of Columbia Lake, source of the mighty Columbia River, near Canal Flats, B.C.
Nicholas Morant Photo/Canadian Pacific Corporate Archives.

(Above) Three Fairbanks-Morse-built diesels with a unit train of Crows Nest coal is seen rolling along the wild Kootenay River at Torrent, above Skookumchuck. This coal traffic saved the Kootenay Central, turning it into CP's busiest branch and leading to a complete track renewal.

Nicholas Morant Photo/Canadian Pacific Corporate Archives

(Below) Waiting for a train at the old Fort Steele station, which has long since disappeared. The only station there now belongs to the Fort Steele Historic Park and has seasonal steam-powered trains.

B.C. Provincial Archives

(Above) Fort Steele is now the site of a historic park and living museum, including steam train rides behind one of three locomotives. Here is 2-6-2 No. 1077, which worked in logging service on Vancouver Island from 1923 until 1969.

(Below) Steamed-up in front of the Fort Steele enginehouse (and seen from the roof) are 3-truck Shay No. 115 (also formerly used for island logging), plus the 1895 Scottish "Dunrobin," built for the Duke of Sutherland, who hauled royal friends in the ornate coach seen on the right.   Both, AHW photos

81

(Above) The historic roundhouse in Cranbrook, B.C. is one of the few such structures left in Canada. On this summer morning in 1986, five classes of Canadian Pacific diesel power are present, including SD40 No. 5547 (GMD 1966), plus (going left): GP38-2 No. 3041 (GMD 1985), GP30 No. 5001 (one of two in Canada, built by GMD in 1963), SD40-2 No. 5797 (GMD 1978), and GP9 No. 8525 (GMD 1955, rebuilt to No. 1644).

(Below) A carman hands up the consist list to conductor of the Kootenay Central wayfreight, headed out of Cranbrook to Golden in 1991, near the end of the caboose era. A pair of GP38's is coming into town from the Crowsnest Pass, while a small part of Cranbrook's railway museum is visible beyond the station.

Both, AHW photos

(Above) Young and old flock to downtown Cranbrook, B.C. for a visit to the world-class Canadian Museum of Rail Travel, where five complete passenger trains from different eras are being assembled and restored. The old C.P.R. station from nearby Elko sits at left.

(Below) Looking from the Elko station at some of the passenger train splendor at Cranbrook's railway museum, including the 1929 dining car "Argyle" and two open-end observation cars.

Both Photos, Mike Westren

(Above) Here's another surviving C.P.R. station, now serving art and cultural functions in Fernie, B.C. The building was still in service during this 1978 visit by the steam-powered B.C. Provincial Museum Train, led by ex-C.P.R. No. 3716.

(Opposite) An eastbound Crowsnest wayfreight crawls slowly up the siding while waiting for a meet with a coal train at the 1901 Canadian Pacific station in Elko, B.C., shortly before the building was closed in 1986 and then moved to Cranbrook.

(Below) New motive power for the Canadian Rockies in the 1990's, as a pair of SD40-2F's waits at Sparwood, B.C. for a crew change, before hauling a mile and a half of empty cars to the Greenhills coal mine on CP Rail's heavy-duty Fording branch.   All Three Photos, AHW

(Above) Downtown Lethbridge, Alberta in 1979 was still dominated by Canadian Pacific's rail yard, although four years later it was torn up and moved, leaving only the station and mainline here, plus the huge viaduct beyond. British Columbia's famous "Royal Hudson" was visiting with a tourism train on this occasion, the last time for a steam whistle to be heard out here on the prairie. Roundhouse and steel water tower are in the distance.

(Below) Last season for the station at Aldersyde, Alberta, as an Extra North from Fort Macleod heads by for Calgary.
Both Photos, AHW

(Above) Prairie grain elevators and prairie wayfreight
combine in this scene at High
River in the summer of 1984.
Beyond the cars on the right
is the old High River station,
made of stone and now a
thriving museum that in-
cludes displays of vintage
C.P.R. trains.   AHW Photo

(Left) The outskirts of High
River in the summer of 1952
see the passing of a passenger
train hauled by proud C.P.R.
"Pacific" No. 2354, the last
steam engine regularly assigned to one engineer, an
old-timer named Bill Barrett.
Jim Hope Photo

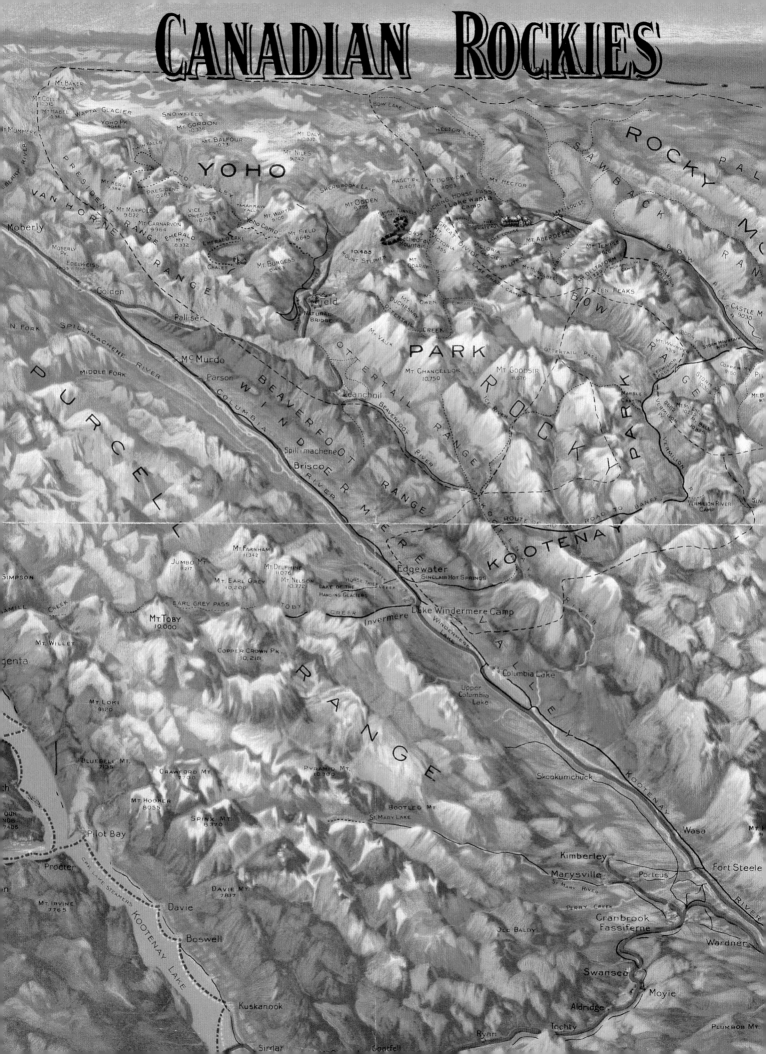

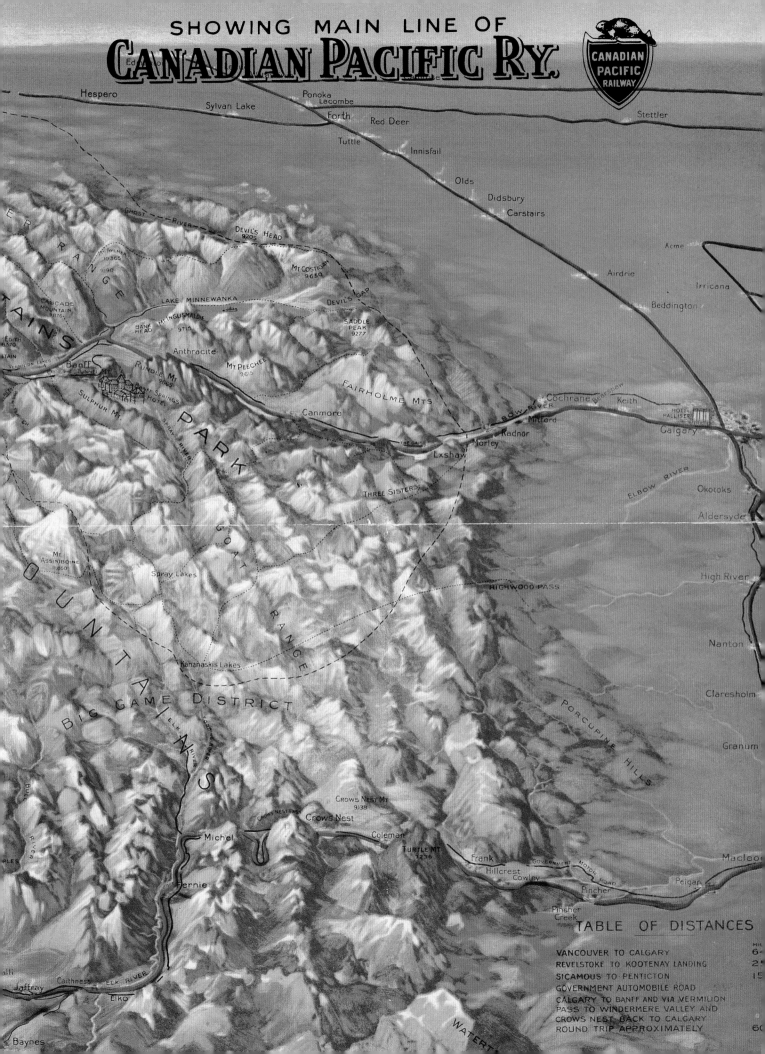

(Above) C.P.R. engineer Clayton Harris checks the time to see when his "Selkirk" might be heading out of Calgary. Alas, both man and machine were already long retired by the time of this 1978 photo. Clayton is gone now, but the engine he often ran rests at Calgary's Heritage Park.
(Below) Downtown Calgary in 1989, during the final season of cabooses and daily passenger service on the Canadian Pacific mainline. The eastbound "Canadian" has 4 diesel units of different types on its head-end.

Both Photos, AHW

(Above) Steam in the Canadian Rockies, back in the days when Calgary's "Selkirk" still ran. This could be her, or one of her mates, rolling eastbound along the Bow River near Banff in 1951, hauling Canada's premier train, the "Dominion." Castle Mountain is in the background.

(Below) Here's one fabulous engine from the Rockies that you can still see - Calgary's "Selkirk" for sure, this time - hauling the westbound "Dominion" near Banff in the 1950's. Upon retirement the engine was renumbered "5934," as in the photo opposite, but she was built as No. 5931.

Both Photos, Nicholas Morant/Canadian Pacific Corporate Archives.

(Above) The "Dominion" is being hauled up Field Hill in the summer of 1951 by "Selkik" 2-10-4 Nos. 5916 and 5925.
Ernie Plant Photo

(Below) It was 30° below zero F. on this February day in 1949 as train No. 2, the "Dominion" headed from Banff towards Calgary.
G.L. Moorhouse Photo

(Above) Even with part of it taken up by a steak and lobster restaurant, the impressive stone-faced station at Banff still had plenty of room in 1988 for those travelling on the daily "Canadian." Note the pairing of old and new diesel power.

(Below) Lake Louise station has also become a fashionable restaurant since this early 1987 shot of train No. 2 during its ten minute stop. The log station remains from stage coach days! Both Photos, AHW

(Above left) Mikado No. 5440 was in charge of the "Dominion" on this summer day at Yoho in 1947.
G.L. Moorhouse Photo

(Above right) Steam was gone from the Canadian Rockies by 1960, when GP9 No. 8687 was recorded at the entrance to the Lower Spiral Tunnel. Mount Cathedral looms in the background.
Nicholas Morant Photo/Canadian Pacific Corporate Archives

(Below) Rare colour scene of the "Mountaineer," a joint C.P.R. - Soo Line train, about to enter the Lower Spiral Tunnel in 1942. Note the open air observation car on the back.   G.L. Moorhouse Photo

(Above) Train No. 1, the westbound "Canadian," winds its way along the Kicking Horse River at Glenogle, B.C. on Sept. 4, 1968.
Lawrence Stuckey Photo

(Below) Fairbanks-Morse-built "C-Liner" No. 4078 leads three General Motors "Geeps" at the head of an upgrade freight on Field Hill in this dramatic scene from the late 1950's.
Nicholas Morant Photo/Canadian Pacific Corporate Archives

(Above) It's the summer of 1948; the afternoon sun shines brightly on the handsome consist of Train No. 8, in charge of "Selkirk" 2-10-4 No. 5926, with Castle Mountain on the distant skyline.

G.L. Moorhouse Photo

(Below) The vintage station at Golden, B.C. used to connect mainline train passengers with steamboats and stagecoaches headed down the Columbia and Kootenay valleys in the early 1900's. Train No. 1, the westbound "Canadian," has just arrived late after crossing the Rockies on this autumn night in 1986. The station was closed soon afterwards, though it has been preserved for historical purposes.

Adolf and Okan Hungry Wolf Photo

• FORT STEELE •

(Above) Crews pose with two of the steam locomotives that operate seasonally at Fort Steele, where the British Columbia government has created a historic interpretive town and park. Big three-truck Shay No. 115 originally worked on Vancouver Island and is a geared engine of the type used by several logging railroads in the Fort Steele area during the early 1900s. Behind is the "Dunrobin," a small 0-4-4 Tanker built in Scotland in 1895 for the Duke of Sutherland.

(Right) Shay No. 115 undergoing heavy repairs in the Fort Steele engine house. The short railway hauls tourists along a sandy bluff overlooking CP's Kootenay Central line. Its roster also includes a Montreal-built 2-6-2 and some vintage rolling stock.

Both, AHW photos

(Above) Downtown Cranbrook looking eastward, circa 1904, with the station at left.

B.C. Provincial Archives

• CRANBROOK •

(Below) Typical turn-of-the-century motive power around Cranbrook was 4-6-0 No. 473, with its oil-burning headlight and a string of wooden cars.

B.C. Provincial Archives

(Above) The Cranbrook roundhouse in the fall of 1916. An early layer of snow covers nearby hillsides. Seven early-day steamers of the East Kootenays stare out from the roundhouse stalls. Steam in back is rising from the boiler room, where power was generated for operating shop machinery. The car shop building is adjacent. Two early stock cars sit in the foreground. Next to them is a gondola filled with cinders dumped by locomotives into the ash pit.

(Below): The car shop building in Cranbrook in 1916. This facility employed a work force that included carpenters, blacksmiths, and machinists. They could build and rebuild most any car used on the railway in those days.

Both Photos/Canadian Pacific Corporate Archives

Collapse of the Cranbrook Station

When the Crow's Nest line was completed in 1897, Cranbrook had a fine, new, two-storey station. But within a few years that station was not big enough for all the business inside of it. Accordingly, the C.P.R. decided to enlarge the station by adding a third storey to it. This was to be done with another floor constructed between the original first and second storey.

Workmen for the project somehow separated the two floors and began to jack up the top floor, while railroad business went on underneath. They got the heavy second floor raised high enough to build the new framework in between. After that they started to remove the support blocks so that the old second storey could be lowered back down on the new one. Everything seemed to be going well when suddenly the whole thing quivered momentarily, then fell northward and crushed the new second floor studding, pinning the workmen in between.

The **Cranbrook Herald** of May 25, 1905, ran this front page story:

"At 10.30 last Tuesday morning the second storey of the C.P.R. station that was being jacked up to admit construction of a third storey fell without a moment's warning, catching all the men working beneath - 11 of them, and all quite badly injured ... Within five minutes ... a great, horror-stricken crowd gathered about the ruins of the depot, anxious to do all in their power to assist the victims of the disaster."

Most bystanders thought all the workmen had surely been killed, but rescuers managed to pull them all out alive. Only one died later, in the hospital. The tragedy could have been a great deal worse. Everyone praised the original builder of the station, because the bottom floor held up so well, even though the whole top crashed down on it. The bottom floor was full of employees and customers. Not only that, but had the building fallen to the west instead of north it might have crushed some of the many passengers waiting on the station platform for the passenger train, which was due momentarily.

Not to be dismayed, railway officials went ahead with the original plans for raising the top story and building a second story underneath. The work was later completed without further mishap, using much of the material salvaged from the accident.

There is some confusion as to the history of Cranbrook's present station, which is a large wooden building along the lines of that fatal rebuilt one, but without its vintage appearance. Some say it is the old station, slightly remodeled, while others say it is a brand new station, built in the architecturally-plain period of the 1940's.

Research finally turned up the story that the C.P.R. wanted to build a new station in the early 40's during the war. At that time, war rationing did not allow the construction of brand new buildings, so the railroad took apart the old station, down to its basic framework, then built the new station over it.

C.P.R. STATION   CRANBROOK, B.C.

1735

(Above) Bunting and flags decorate the Cranbrook station, while dignitaries and officials wait on the platform for the arrival of this special train drawn by shiny No. 5108, thought to be carrying a royal visitor sometime in the 1930's.   Nicholas Morant Photo/Canadian Pacific Corporate Archives

CANADIAN
PACIFIC

TRANS-CANADA
LIMITED

WORLD'S
GREATEST
TRAVEL
SYSTEM

(Above) Another special train at Cranbrook shows spotless No. 1206 with cars carrying C.P.R. President W.M. Neal on his 1947 system-wide inspection tour. Meanwhile, the original appearance of the town's station has been greatly altered by remodeling, although part of the original frame remains within this "new" structure. Canadian Pacific Corporate Archives

(Below): Looking southward at the station in 1949, as cars for the Kootenay Central mixed wait for the rest of their train. Paterson-George Collection

(Above) Steam power returned briefly to Cranbrook in the spring of 1979 with the arrival of former CPR "Royal Hudson" No. 2860 during its trip through the Canadian Rockies to promote tourism for the B.C. government. Large crowds turned out to see the engine and its maroon train during a two-day layover and display by the station, though hardly anyone was on hand while the engine "stretched its legs" and blew off steam in this early morning view. In the years since this visit, Cranbrook has become home to its own maroon train - the restored "Trans-Canada Limited" - centerpiece of the world-class Canadian Museum of Rail Travel, which will include at least two preserved C.P.R. steam locomotives at an impressive trackside setting starting just behind where this photo was taken.

AHW Photo

(Above) This view of Cranbrook's railway yard was taken from the tender of the "Royal Hudson" during its 1979 visit and shows the station, future museum site (which includes the buildings beyond) and the old roundhouse on the distant right, which is also expected to become part of future historical developments.

(Below) Motive power at Cranbrook in the winter of 1978 included this visitor from the Union Pacific Railroad, which makes connections with CP Rail at Kingsgate, 51 miles to the south.

Both, AHW Photos

(Above) Arrival of the famed "Soo Flyer" at Moyie in 1908. Coming from Seattle via Spokane, this express train served several Canadian locations on its way east, before it went back into the U.S. and on to St. Paul and Chicago. The Canadian Museum of Rail Travel in Cranbrook is restoring an example of this train for display.

B.C. Provincial Archives

From Spokane to Banff via Cranbrook in 1911

When Owen Moon, Jr. wrote to the C.P.R. in 1911 and said that he wanted to go to Banff from Spokane, the instructions he received from the company agent would discourage most modern travelers from making the trip. Since Mr. Moon was an editor for the Trenton Evening Times in New Jersey, we can assume that the C.P.R. was anxious to send him home with a good report. Here is what they told him:

"Dear Sir...(we) note that you wish to reach the main line of the C.P.R. West of Banff, coming up from Spokane. I think if you intend to take this trip, that you should come-up to Curzon and get off at Cranbrook on the Crow's Nest Branch of the C.P.R. A stage travels through the Kootenay and Columbia Valleys and is one of the most beautiful stage routes in British Columbia.

"According to your remarks, I should imagine that it is *your intention to take ladies with you, and would point out that at this season of the year, it is rather a hard trip for a lady by stage for 150 miles. You can, however, hire a motor car at Cranbrook which would cost you $25.00 per day and you could make the run at the outside, in a day and a half. Going by this route, you will arrive at Golden on the main line of the C.P.R.*

The only other route to take would be to come to Curzon, take the train on the Crow's Nest branch going West, to Kootenay Landing, from there get boat to Nelson (the boat meets the train). From Nelson take train to Robson, where steamer meets the train, and go from that point to Arrowhead, traveling all day through the Upper and Lower Arrow Lakes. From Arrowhead, it is just a short run by rail to Revelstoke, on the main line of the Canadian Pacific Railway..."

(Above) Along Moyie Lake, a few miles south of Cranbrook, lies the old mining town of Moyie, where a Kootenay Indian discovered a rich galena outcrop in 1893 leading to an important lead-silver mine that helped bring the railway. Here's the special "Royal Hudson" train at Moyie in 1979.

(Below): One year earlier another special train toured the area behind former CPR 2-8-0 No. 3716, seen here at the Moyie Tunnel on the shores of Moyie Lake, with a CP Rail diesel in the lead.

Both, AHW Photos

(Above) Hauling the Kettle Valley and Crow's Nest passenger train in July 1947 was 4-6-2 No. 1233, seen during its stop at Yahk, B.C.   W.C. Whittaker Photo

(Below) The same train and location is seen one year earlier with engine No. 1205.   W.C. Whittaker Photo

(Opposite, Top) "Royal Hudson" No. 2860 is making a brief stop at Yahk during a late-spring snow-storm in 1979. The 1912 station was torn down three years later.   AHW Photo

(Opposite, Below) A load of ore rolls north along the Moyie River near Yahk in 1979.   AHW Photo

(Above) Kimberley's 1902 station as it looked in 1948. It has been preserved at this location.

Ralph Manning Photo

• Kimberley, B.C. •

(Below) Kimberley's Sullivan Mine was discovered in 1892 and grew to be one of the world's largest lead-zinc mines. Seen here in the 1920s, it provided major traffic for many years over CP's 18.7 mile Kimberley branch.

Canadian Pacific Corporate Archives

(Above) The Sullivan Mine was taken over by Cominco in 1909. The operation included some 45 miles of 3-foot gauge electric railroad, all but 4 miles of it underground. This scene was taken more than a mile down, in November 1947.   Nicholas Morant Photo/Canadian Pacific Corporate Archives

(Below) Heaviest power on Cominco's narrow gauge electric railway included No. 102, a 28-ton machine equipped with air brakes and operated from the overhead 220 volt wires. Lighter engines lacked air brakes and ran from their own battery systems. A heavy train consisted of 40 loaded cars weighing 25 tons each. Grades were up to 2%, with train movements monitored by a central dispatcher and signal lighting.   Cominco Photo

Crow's Nest Pass Lumber Company

JOHN BRECKENRIDGE, PRESIDENT.   WILLIAM CARLIN, VICE PRESIDENT.   PETER LUND, MANAGING DIRECTOR, SEC. AND TREAS.

Crow's Nest Pass Lumber Company, Ltd.

TELEGRAPHIC ADDRESS,
CROWLUMBER, WARDNER, B.C.

CODES USED,
AMERICAN LUMBER TELECODE.
A. B. C. FOURTH EDITION.

Wardner,
BRITISH COLUMBIA,

(Opposite) There were a number of logging railroads in the Canadian Rockies, mainly between Golden and the U.S. border, including the Shay and Heisler-powered Crow's Nest Lumber Company seen on these pages. The CNL operated railroad branches off the CPR's Kootenay Central line at several places around Wasa and Skookumchuck, bringing trains of logs out to the interchanges for the CPR to haul away. Geared locomotives were preferred for the rough tracks.

(Opposite, Centre) A builder's portrait of Heisler No. 3, the "Will Baker," in 1920.

(Opposite, Below) A two-truck Shay, a homemade loading car, and a string of logs.   AHW Collection

(This Page) Two views of the Crow's Nest Pass Lumber Company's impressive mill at Wardner, along the Kootenay River and the C.P.R. Crow's Nest line.   Glenbow-Alberta Institute

(Above) Bull River is the setting for this photo of CP Rail No. 8721 leading a string of coal cars in January of 1973. The engine's white exhaust indicates cold weather - it was -30°F!   Grant B. Will Photo

(Below) Crew and station agent pose in front of the Jaffray, B.C. station with a mixed train led by No. 3218. Everything in this 1915 scene is long gone, with Jaffray no longer listed in CP Rail timetables.
John Paulsen Photo

Building through the Crow's Nest Pass

"The Directors feel that they cannot too strongly urge the immediate construction of a line from Lethbridge to a connection with your Columbia & Kootenay Railway at Nelson, a distance of 325 miles, and anticipating your approval they have already taken steps toward commencement of the work on the opening of spring ...

The interests of the country at large are so much concerned in this question that your Directors confidently expect reasonable assistance at the hands of the Dominion Government."

From the C.P.R. Annual Report of 1896.

South-eastern British Columbia's wilderness region was known to consist of many minerals. There was great potential for profit-making by those who could mine the minerals and for those who could haul the mined minerals to world-wide markets. By the 1880's the area was being harvested for quantities of gold, silver, copper, lead, and zinc. That was during the time when great wealth was being made and spent in building railway lines to previously wild and remote regions. It became only a matter of which railway company would be the first to reach the Crow's Nest area when the C.P.R. made the above statement to its shareholders.

Because of the north to south run of the mountains, rivers and valleys around the Kootenay region, it seemed the avenues of transportation might develop the same way. Since the region lies next to the U.S. border, American interests were the first to begin developing the Crow's Nest region. The closest American rival to the C.P.R. was the transcontinental Great Northern Railway, which was built from St. Paul Minnesota to Seattle, Washington. The Great Northern's branch lines slowly crawled into British Columbia, with one branch approaching the Crow's Nest area. In 1895 this branch reached Nelson. The following year the C.P.R. got to work on a line of its own.

The Canadian government signed an agreement with the C.P.R., in which the railway promised to build a line from Lethbridge to Nelson via the Crow's Nest Pass. The government promised to subsidize the railway at the rate of $11,000 for each mile of that line. This came to nearly three and a half million dollars, a lot of money in the 1890's. The price was raised in part because the C.P.R. also promised to reduce its freight rates for the benefit of farmers, consumers, and the country's finances. Among the goods receiving low rates were to be grain and flour, headed to eastern markets from the prairies, and farm implements heading west, the other way. Of course, government coffers would also grow tremendously with the development brought by the railway line.

The C.P.R. got another bonus for building the Crow's Nest Pass line from the Provincial government of British Columbia. Back in 1888 the B.C. legislature chartered a rail line from the provincial boundary in the Crow's Nest to the Kootenays. This new railway would receive 20,000 acres of provincial land for every mile built, plus six square miles of coal lands in the Crow's Nest Pass region. On paper the chartered line was first known as the Crow's Nest and Kootenay Lake Railway Company. Later it was renamed the British Columbia Southern Railway, but it remained on paper until the C.P.R. made its 1896 announcement and commenced building the line as a branch of its own company. Thus it qualified for the charter and its gifts.

Construction of the C.P.R.'s Crow's Nest Pass line - the B.C. Southern Railway - gave the company 3.75 million acres of land, for which it eventually got 1.8 million dollars. By 1901, the area provided the C.P.R. with 112,000 tons of coal and 199,000 tons of coke to carry. And this amount did not include anything from the six square miles of coal lands that the company was given for building the new line. In 1897 it had made an agreement to haul for the Crow's Nest Pass Coal Company all its freight, in return for not doing any coal mining of its own in the area for ten years.

(Above) Elko at the turn-of-the-century was quite a busy town, with several stores and hotels. Parked in front of the station here, we see an early-model pile driver that was used in building bridges and trestles along the line.
B.C. Provincial Archives

• ELKO •

(Below) C-Liner No. 4104 roars past Elko with an Extra West. Operator H.J. Wharton has just passed the order hoop up to the brakeman in the cab window.
Grant B. Will Photo

(Above) The Crow's Nest Way freight waits for a meet with an eastbound through freight at Elko Station in 1978. This building now sits in the heart of Cranbrook as part of the impressive Canadian Museum of Rail Travel.

AHW Photo

Working on the Railway Gang Over Crow's Nest Pass in 1898

By James Compton
(From the *Creston Review*)

"When one considers all the now old fashioned tools and equipment used on that 18 month job, we of today must consider it as super remarkable. Those hard rock drillers of 1897-98 had no machine drills. It was all hand drilling, and, in the very windy Crow's Nest Pass, the rock drillers were often obliged to lay off, because, when the wind was heaviest and very gusty, there was the danger of an unbalanced miss-stroke, injuring or even killing the drill holder.

For the earth work, slip and wheeled scrapers were hauled by horses, but, in long earth hauls, a track was laid, and small one-yard dump cars were used and filled by hand shovels, then hauled by a single horse. In some places where sufficient earth was along the road bed, the work was let out by contract, in station lengths, to men who did the work with shovels picks and wheel barrows.

As for getting in supplies of food for men, horses and mules, and for powder and other materials, a tote road was built from Kuskanook to Crows Nest. All supplies came either from the Kootenay Lake section, via steam boat down the Kootenay every day from Jennings, Montana, or to Wardner, B.C., or from the Eastern section by rail or wagon from Lethbridge.

Practically every mile of the way from Pincher Creek to Wardner and from Cranbrook to the Kootenay Lake was heavily timbered virgin country, with much of it requiring heavy rock cutting, several tunnels, and innumerable bridges and trestles.

During the warm months there were mosquitoes in abundance, with neither screens or spray appliances. To these were added lice and other undesirables. The food was plainest, with not much choice.

To some extent, these hardships were overcome as soon as trains were able to run. This work train supply service was put on as soon as the grade was wide enough to hold the ties and rails; and temporary skeleton bridges permitted the bringing in of steam shovels, to widen and complete the road bed. Also with them would come the pile drivers to install permanent bridges.

..The death toll from sickness was very much greater than from accident. Especially at Crow's Nest and Goat River Crossing one would expect the loss of life would be great in the spring floods, but I know of no cases of drowning.

The C.P.R. had just completed a sawmill along the Elk River, a little west of Fernie, when much damage was done by high water. Bridges were washed out just when completed. A couple of bridges were also burned out at the Crow's Nest Loop.

We reached Wardner in August when the Kootenay water was lowering. Even then, the men had to work in water up to their waists at times, to get the steel across as soon as possible. In part, this hurry was because some of the contractors were finished with their contracts and were waiting to ship their equipment west to another hurry up job.

I had been paying $2 per day for a room in the hotel, but as soon as the trains got across, taking the grade crews to the next work further west, the hotel was so empty one might have rented the whole building for $2.

As to working hours, there was no thought of a mere 8 hour day. Twelve and fourteen hours were common, and on some urgent cases, some worked forty-eight hours without a stop except for meals.

For a ten hour day on bridge work, we got $2.75, with over-time and Sunday work, double pay.

We were driving piling, when about 4 p.m., a pulley broke on top of the pile driver, which was about 110 feet high. It was getting dark and cold, about 30 degrees below zero, and the strong wind was swaying the pile driver, when the boss said to me, 'Jim, I guess it's up to you to go up an change that broken pulley.'

There was no light except for a shadow-flinging wood fire on the ground while I climbed up and did the job. I thought while doing it - if I ever get down alive - I'll quit! Then, when I got down safely, I thought I should have quit before I went up. But I stayed on.

Towns grew fast with the laying of the steel. Macleod, Alberta was the headquarters. At that time there was still visible, the remains of the old North West Mounted Police fort which had been built of logs. It seemed a strange place to have built a fort. The place was infested with rattlesnakes.

Cowley, Blairmore, Coleman or Coaldale were unknown then. We reached Crow's Nest, then known as Bulls Head, and where the waters of the lake flow both ways, to the Pacific and Atlantic oceans. The steel arrived at Fernie in July 1898, and the first freight bill, if I remember correctly, was for $5,000 on the fire brick for coke ovens which can still be seen beside the tracks.

Fernie really boomed from then on for some time. I well remember being in Fernie on July 12, 1898. It was a very hot day and the best place we could find to sleep that night was in a box car which was loaded with steel rails. They were hard, but we were tired and slept well.

There was nothing at Elko, but Wardner was lively because of the daily steamboat service from Jennings, Montana. Cranbrook soon became a thriving center - diverted from Fort Steele. Fort Steele had been the Wild Horse gold town of the Kootenays from the 1860's onward and much wealth had been taken from the creek in placer gold: but it was now passed by and Cranbrook became the big center .."

119

(Above) Part of downtown Fernie after the great fire that destroyed most of the buildings. The train in the background sits near the smoldering ruins of the C.P.R. station.   K.C. Baker Collection

The Fernie Fire of 1908

"Scorched and blistered by whirling flames, blinded by smoke, dust and ashes, crazed by separation from loved ones and fleeing they knew to whither, checked by walls of flame just as safety seemed at hand, confused by the suddenness of the catastrophe and faint with seemingly futile exertion, the people of Fernie went through an experience that will be remembered with horror as long as they live.

The swiftest horse that ever looked through a bridge could not gallop as fast as that fire leaped and hurled itself from building to building."

So read an article in **The Fernie Free Press**, after the fire was over. Most of the town was destroyed, with loss of life and property that affected everyone. Had it not been for the railway trains, those losses would have been much greater yet.

The eastbound passenger train of the C.P.R. was ordered to leave all its passengers at Elko and to proceed empty to Fernie in order to carryout those who wanted to go. As soon as it was filled up, the train backed down to Elko and dropped off its load, then headed up to Fernie for more. Several trips were made, with the train filled to capacity each time.

Meanwhile, the Great Northern Railway had two locomotives steamed up in Fernie. Coupled together, these two hooked on to all the cars they could handle, which were quickly filled with fleeing people. This train raced out of town and to a cutbank along the Elk River, where the people were able to wait out the fire in safety.

When the fire was finally over the people of Fernie went back to salvage what they could, and to rebuild the rest. The C.P.R. freight agent, showing typical company allegiance of the period, went back to the charred railway yards and dug up $2,800 of his company's money that he had hurriedly buried before leaving.

(Above) C.P.R. 4-4-0 No. 34 has arrived at Fernie's new station with the first through train from Medicine Hat in 1898.
Canadian Pacific Corporate Archives

(Below) An early Mogul (2-6-0) type engine with a westbound freight train at Fernie in 1902. The buildings in this scene were all destroyed during later fires.
British Columbia Provincial Archives

(Above) The Fernie station and water tower back in the years when trains made regular stops here.

Warren Rohn Photo

(Below) No. 2640 sits by the Fernie water tower in 1945, when the town still depended heavily on the daily train services.

R.V. Nixon Photo

(Above) Consolidation No. 3741 has finished at the Fernie water tank and is ready to continue to Cranbrook.

• FERNIE •

(Below) A doubleheaded freight led by Nos. 3712 and 3600 has stopped for water at Fernie in this 1940's scene.

Both photos, Warren Rohn

Crow's Nest Railroading with "Corky" O'Rourke

Told at the Fernie Station in 1978

"I came from the west to work out here in the Rockies in 1947. I went to Michel first, then moved here to Fernie in March of 1948. I've seen a lot of changes around this old station in the thirty years since then. This was an important place. All the trains were still pulled by steam. We never saw any diesels until sometime in 1951. The roads in these mountains weren't too dependable, especially in the winters. There was no airline service. Lots of people traveled by train. The trains carried the mail and the express parcels. They hauled fresh food that had to reach the markets in a hurry. They hauled the dead to the last resting places.

There was often several dozen people around this station in my early years working here, especially when the passenger trains came in. We had four of them scheduled daily - two each way. There was the Night Train that was known as the Kettle Valley run. It was pretty much a first rate train, with dining car and sleepers besides coaches, baggage cars, and express cars. This was Train 11 and 12, from Medicine Hat clear across B.C. to Vancouver. You could go from Fernie to the coast in about 28 hours. In those days it took nearly as long by car, but it was a much rougher ride. Parts of the highway weren't paved, and some of it was pretty rugged going.

(Below) "Corky" O'Rourke at his desk inside Fernie station in 1978, not long before his retirement and the station's closing.

AHW Photo

(Above) Engineer George Hannon watches from the cab of former C.P.R. 2-8-0 No. 3716 as "Corky" O'Rourke hands up a hoop with the "orders" at the Fernie station in 1978. The station has been moved back from here a few feet to serve the town in its new role as art center.

AHW Photo

"Later on they changed trains 11 and 12 to number 45 and 46, and they used diesels for power. But even after they dieselized, I recall times when they had to put steam on the front end to pull them through. There were times when the riverbanks would overflow and flood the tracks. That would short out the diesel-electric motors, so they had to pull them through with steam. When business started dropping off they replaced the passenger train with a Dayliner - those self-propelled cars built by Budd.

The other train for passengers that still ran when I came here was a mixed. It hauled freight from Yahk to Lethbridge, daily, with a coach and baggage car on the back for passengers. Of course, it wasn't very fast, since it stopped along the way and did some switching. But it wasn't as bad as some of the other locals near here - like the one from Cranbrook to Kimberley, that often took five hours for the twenty mile trip., Engine 975 was regularly assigned to the Yahk-Lethbridge Mixed.

In those days this station provided a lot of services. For instance, this next room was the telegraph office. A lot of people didn't have phones, so they sent telegrams when they wanted to get a message off in a hurry. That service was available six days a week here and it employed a telegraph agent, a telegraph messenger and a delivery boy. The big, heavy desk that they used is in their office, yet. You could hear the morse code of their equipment all day long.

Then, in the other end of the building was the express office. It was in charge of an express agent, and he had his own men working for him. Another name for the express shipments was fast freight. Regular freight was shipped on freight cars, because it was big and heavy. But if somebody had smaller shipments that they wanted to get to someplace in a hurry, they could send it on the express car with the passenger train. That was almost overnight delivery from Alberta to the coast.

"Frozen meat and chickens were usually shipped in refrigerated express cars as part of the passenger trains. Wednesdays and Thursdays there were always fresh loads of fish brought in from the coast, for the Catholics to eat on Fridays. Live chickens were sent by express, too. One time one of the express boys dropped a box of chickens and it broke. He spent quite a while trying to catch all the chickens running around in the station.

Finally there was the Railway Agent, who looked after the train operations - handled freight, sold tickets, and so on. He lived with his family upstairs, here, and this was the main office for his crew - telegraphers, operators, and assistant agents. Our office was open 24 hours a day, seven days a week.

These express boys usually had bunks where they slept in the express office. About once a month or so they'd come into the station office, here, and sit around most of the night, drinking coffee and talking with us. For a long time I wondered about that, until I found out they did that every time there was a corpse waiting in their office to be shipped on the next train. We've been lucky around here in that we've never had any real accidents or disasters, especially around the station. Of course, there have been collisions and derailments out on the line. In 1970 there was a head-on collision just a little ways out of Crow's Nest in which one of the engineers died. The other engineer had overlooked a train order warning him of a superior train, and he had no radio on his engine. A couple of times they've had cars get away, up on the mountain, and not long ago even a diesel engine. Back in '35 there were 17 cars of coke that ran way and headed downhill for Fernie. Someone opened a switch ahead of them and they piled up into a hill before they got to where there were too many people. About 1960 a single loaded coal car got away like that and made it right down to the Fernie Wye, where somebody opened the switch so it would hit the hill instead of the town. They say it was going 100 miles an hour when it got splattered.

We had some bad winters in my early years, too. One time both Numbers 11 and 12 - the passenger trains - were buried under snow for nearly a week. One was stuck at Sentinel, the other one was just barely out of Crow's Nest. Back in those days they depended mostly on men and shovels to get out of such a mess. Nowadays they have bulldozers and earth movers and so on. And if they figure a train's going to have a hard time, they put some more diesels on beforehand. They get some strong winds down around Elko. The hotshot freight, No. 980, was buried there for about a week, once."

(Left) Signs of the past near the Fernie station in 1978.
AHW Photo

(Above) Looking westward from the Fernie station and water tower in June 1949, waiting for the passenger train to pull in. This is now one of the finer preserved stations in Western Canada.

Paterson-George Collection

(Above) No. 8728 heads five units built by the Canadian Locomotive Company on eastbound train No. 78 at Sparwood in March, 1973.
(Below) C-Liners 4053 and 4104 are crossing the overhead bridge at McGillivray in July 1973.

Both Photos, Grant B. Will

(Above) A modern unit train at the Byron Creek coal loading facility at Corbin, B.C. A coal contract with Ontario Hydro caused C.P. Rail to rebuild the old Eastern British Columbia Railway line from McGillivray to Corbin.

Nicholas Morant Photo/Canadian Pacific Corporate Archives

(Above and Below) Two views of Michel at the turn of the century, showing the coal works, company town, station, and railway yards.

B.C. Provincial Archives

(Above) A little 0-4-0 Dinkey engine switches coking cars at Michel's coal and coke plant in November, 1947. This engine is now on display in Fernie.
(Below) Caboose of an outbound coal train looks back at the Michel yard in this dramatic 1962 scene.

Both Photos, Nicholas Morant/Canadian Pacific Corporate Archives

(Above) Highest point on Crow's Nest line is here at Crow's Nest. This 1906 view shows the station at its original location on the edge of Crow's Nest Lake. It was replaced in 1907 with the larger building seen below.

(Below) Train time at Crow's Nest station in 1924.   Both Photos, Canadian Pacific Corporate Archives

(Above) For many years Mikado (2-8-2) No. 5149 was based at Crow's Nest to perform switching in the yard and at nearby coal plants. In this 1953 view, the engine is seen leaving the servicing area.
Photo by Michael Woodhead

• CROWSNEST •

(Below) Another long-time regular in the Crow's Nest area was 2-8-0 No. 3758, seen here near the shops on September 16, 1945.
R. V. Nixon Photo

(Above) Train No. 67 from Nelson to Medicine Hat was stopped at Crow's Nest in 1951 to pick up passengers and express.

W.C. Whittaker Photo

(Below) Several diesel models idled on the ready-track during this late-winter day in 1978, including GP-9's, SD-40's, and a lone F9 B-unit. Note the leased "Precision" Geep.

AHW Photo

(Above) Sperry Rail Service operates some of the most antique railroad equipment in the Canadian Rockies during its twice-a-year (or so) inspection of CP Rail lines. SRS No. 119 is one of 18 similar vehicles used by Sperry as it searches electronically for hidden flaws in the rails. One part of the self-propelled car is equipped with modern instruments while the crew lives in another part. Now diesel-powered, these cars were first operated in the 1920's and 30's as rapid-transit passenger carriers, equipped with gas-electric motors and owned by several lines in the eastern U.S. a way-freight is just coming in from Fort Macleod with a GP-9, a tank car and a caboose.

AHW Photo

(Above) This interesting covered bridge was located just outside of Blairmore in 1912. Crow's Nest Mountain is in the background. Fire dangers made covered bridges obsolete in most places years ago.

Glenbow-Alberta Institute

Towns and Stations of the Crow's Nest Pass

The famous Father DeSmet hiked through the Crow's Nest Pass in 1845 and became the first to take note of the area's coal deposits. Since then, countless mines and miners have worked seams of black rock between Elko, on the west, and Lundbreck, on the east - the general region of Crow's Nest Pass. At first, this work was small-scale and sporadic, but after the C.P.R. built a line through the Pass, it became the major occupation.

Many citizens of the area wanted the federal government to build and control the Crow's Nest rail line, after it was first proposed in the early 1880's. When other private companies showed interest in doing so, the Alberta Railway & Coal Company reminded them of its first claim by publishing the following notice in the **Lethbridge News.**

"Notice is hereby given that Alberta Railway & Coal Company are applying to Parliament to revive the powers given to it under section 5330, to extend and operate its railway from Lethbridge to Hope (B.C.) by way of Fort Macleod through Crow's Nest Pass and giving it powers to operate branch lines. A. Ferguson, Solicitor for Applicant."

Fernie was the first town to boom after the railway was built. It's name came from two mine developers, the Fernie Brothers. The Crow's Nest Pass Coal Company already had a mine in operation at nearby Coal Creek. Plans called for other mines to be built and for Fernie to serve as the center of them. The Morrissey, Fernie & Michel Railway was to connect those three towns for the benefit of the coal business. By January 1899 smoke was billowing from fifty new coke ovens at Fernie and there were plans to build another 150 or 200. By December 15, 1904 the Great Northern Railway reached Fernie under the name of the Crow's Nest Southern Railway. The town's population was getting near 2,000.

But the quick build-up did not come without its accompanying disasters. On May 22, 1902 an explosion at the Coal Creek mine killed 128 of the 800 men employed there. Two years later a fire roared through Fernie and destroyed six complete blocks., In 1904 several more blocks burnt down during a fire started by careless brush burning along the railroad tracks. Then on August 1, 1908, a forest fire raced into the town and destroyed practically every building, taking ten lives with it. After that the town was rebuilt of concrete and brick

In 1899 another coal mine was opened 25 miles northeast of Fernie, at Michel. Michel was the nickname of Michael Phillips, an early Indian trader who turned prospector and worked in the area. The coal at Michel was of excellent quality and easy to reach, so the mine was expanded quite rapidly. The coal company built houses for its employees near the mine and rented them out for low prices. Michel was a "company town." There were several on the B.C. side of the Crow's Nest, though they were illegal in Alberta.

As the mines at Michel continued to grow, some of the miners moved further west than the company property and began to build their own town. For a while this place was called New Michel, then Newtown and Newton, until 1909, when the C.P.R. named it Natal on its maps for reasons now lost. As Michel and Natal continued to grow they finally fused with each other. The old company houses continued to stand until recent years, giving tourists a glance at a desolate worn-out coal community as they drove by on Highway 3 - the "main street" in the very narrow mountain valley.

The old, wooden tipple at Michel was destroyed by fire in 1937, so the company built a new one of concrete and steel. They also built 20 coking ovens that yielded such coal by-products as tar and gas, in addition to coke. Coal production was so good at Michel that for many years the plant averaged 2,200 tons a day only because there was a shortage of manpower. In 1946 this shortage brought about the introduction of now controversial strip mining techniques. The giant Kaiser Coal Company moved into nearby coal fields and used these techniques on a massive scale.

The coal seams run slightly different on the east side of Crow's Nest Pass, thus many more towns grew up there. At one time there were ten, each with its own mine. While Blairmore might be considered the main one today, the town of Frank was originally the center of activity. For a long time it was the only stop along the new railway, on that side. All business came to a standstill when the daily train arrived.

The town was named for H.L. Frank of Butte, Montana, who formed the Canadian American Company to develop mines in the Crow's Nest. In September of 1901 he chartered a special train to bring guests to the grand opening of his new townsite. Among them was Premier F.G. Haultain of the North West Territories.

In 1903 came the disastrous landslide for which Frank is now best known. However, the slide seems to have caused less harm to the growing town than is commonly thought. The mine was back in production within a few months, and by 1906 the town had a population of nearly 1,000 persons. A nearby sulphur hot springs was turned into a luxury resort, and Alberta's only smelter was built by the Canadian Metal Company. However, in 1911 the government gave an order for the town to be moved across the railroad line out of the way of any further possible landslides. Then, in 1917 a serious gas explosion destroyed the mines to such an extent that they were never rebuilt, so the townspeople slowly moved away.

For a few years Frank was the junction point of the C.P.R. and a shortline called the Frank & Grassy Mountain Railway. This line ran north to the mining town of Lille (named after a town in France by its French developers), seven miles from Frank. The line climbed a steep and narrow canyon and was said to have crossed somewhere between 15 and 30 trestles on the way. In addition to hauling coal and supplies, the shortline's trains took miners and their families back and forth in a caboose. The operation was closed down by the time of the first world war.

Nearby Blairmore began with a log cabin store opened in 1899 by Harry Lyon. At that time the place was known as "Tenth Siding" on C.P.R. maps, and later it was called The Springs, because of a nearby hot sulphur spring. Finally the C.P.R. built a small station of logs and called it Blairmore, in honor of the Hon. A.G. Blair, who was then Minister of Railways. The second C.P.R. agent was Mr. Lyon, the local shopkeeper, who also became the town's first mayor. By then Blairmore had a school, skating rink, church, two hotels, and electric power from Frank. In 1906 the Rocky Mountain Cement Company built a plant there, and in 1911 the Greenhill Mine was opened and became a mainstay of the town's economy.

Coleman had the only coal seam between Blairmore and the B.C. boundary, so two coal mines were developed there. The place was then known as McGillivray's Hill, but the president of one of the companies renamed it for his daughter, Florence Coleman Flumerfelt. History did not record why he didn't call the town Florence or Flumerfelt, instead. By 1906, besides coal shipments from the two mines, the C.P.R. handled four carloads of lime daily from the Crow's Nest Lime Company, and thousands of board feet of lumber from McLaren's Mill, which employed 30 men. In 1910 Coleman became a town when it annexed nearby "Slavtown."

A short distance east of Frank was the station for Hillcrest, which served the large and busy Hillcrest Mines, nearby. This place was named for the mine's founder and promoter, C.P. Hill. It was the site of the worst disaster in the Pass - an explosion in 1914 that killed 189 men. It was the worst mining accident in Canada and the third in the world, at the time. Special railway equipment was brought in to help with the rescue work. However, the mine was reopened and continued to operate until 1949, when its entrances were purposely sealed with dynamite.

The next stop after Hillcrest was Bellevue, which had two coal mines in operation for some years. One of them was the site of the area's first great mine explosion, which claimed thirty men in 1910. Bellevue is French for "beautiful view", and the name was given to it by one of the French mining bosses.

A station called Passburg was the official entrance to the Crow's Nest Pass, and just beyond it was a bustling mining camp called Burmis. Until the coal mine was built in 1912, the place was just a flag stop called Livingstone. It was then renamed in honor of two nearby ranchers, R.H.Y. Burn and Jack Kemmis. However, the coal turned out to be a poor quality, so Burmis faded out until 1938, when the Burmis Lumber Company Limited began operating there.

(Above) This photograph was made at the old coal plant in Coleman around 1912. It shows a C.P.R. work train with a steam shovel, an early 3-window caboose, and a light 2-8-0 engine.

(Below) The narrow gauge mining railway at Coleman in 1912. These fireless engines were known as "thermos bottles" because of the way they used hot steam which was pumped into them frequently from the mine's huge steam boiler.

Both Photos, Glenbow-Alberta Institute

(Above) A load of coal ready to leave Coleman for the Pacific coast in 1967.

Nicholas Morant Photo/Canadian Pacific Corporate Archives

(Below) The Coleman operation during its final seasons in 1978, with the coal company's green switcher at work in the yard. AHW Photo

(Above) Blairmore Station as it looked around the turn of the century, with no tracks yet layed out in front. The small freight shed was an earlier station. The photo was taken from the window of a passing train.   Glenbow-Alberta Institute

The Crow's Nest Train Robbery

It happened aboard train No. 68 during the summer of 1920. Three men bought tickets in Lethbridge, bound for the Crow's Nest flag stop of Sentinel. Conductor Sam Jones told Engineer George Alexander at Coleman that three passengers were to get off at Sentinel. He didn't know that by then they would be on the run.

Jones first noticed that something was amiss when one of the robbers stuck a pistol in his face. At the same time the other two stood up, waving another pistol and telling the passengers to put up their hands and give up their valuables. While the robbers collected the booty, several men passed their wallets to their wives. A quick-thinking power company manager hid $1,000 behind a seat cushion. The robbers got $300 and the conductor's watch, which he had just bought a couple of weeks before for $97. They also got a lot of trouble for their efforts.

The robbery was not a well-planned one. The three men had not disguised themselves nor their heavy foreign accents. Before long, the police were looking for Tom Bassoff, Alex Auloff, and George Akoff. Within the week they found two of them sitting together in a cafe at Bellevue.

When the policemen tried to arrest the robbers at their tables, a gunfight erupted which left two policemen and one robber dead, the other wounded. The wounded one managed to escape. When word reached Lethbridge, a special train was quickly loaded with armed policemen and civilians. It covered the 87 miles from Lethbridge to Frank in slightly more than two hours, which was a record run.

The posse was less than successful. The wounded robber was not found, but during the search one of the armed civilians was shot and killed by another. He had gone into an old shack to look around and then had decided to climb back out through a window, where he was mistaken for the wanted man.

The wounded robber was finally captured near Pincher Creek a few days later, carrying two revolvers. The engineer of an eastbound train had spotted him in his headlight and brought railway police back out with him to make a search. This man was hanged a couple of months later.

The third robber had disappeared after the night of his train ride to Sentinel. He had gone down to the States with his share of the loot, including the conductor's watch. Four years later the watch turned up in a Portland, Oregon pawn shop. The man who pawned it gave information which led to the arrest of Auloff in Butte, Montana. He spent the next seven years in prison, and the conductor got his watch back.

140

Frank Slide, Alberta

(Left) A westbound freight rolls past the town of Frank in 1978, overshadowed by the famous Turtle Mountain, seventy-five years after its rocky face slid down and caused a disaster.   AHW Photo

(Below) Back in 1903, track workers take a pause while rebuilding mine tracks that had been buried by the Frank Slide a few weeks earlier. Both photos on this page show a similar part of Turtle Mountain.

Glenbow-Alberta Institute

(Above) Lundbreck Falls along the Crow's Nest River, with caboose of a westbound rolling off the bridge.

AHW Photo

(Below) C-Liner No. 4065 with Train No. 72, east of Cowley, Alberta, on its way to Lethbridge in 1973.

Grant B. Will Photo

(Above) The C.P.R. Crow's Nest line missed Pincher Creek by about 2 miles, stopping instead at Pincher Station seen here soon after construction in 1897.
(Below) Blizzards in the Rocky Mountain foothill country were among the C.P.R.'s greatest operating challenges. The line was closed due to heavy snow at Pincher station in this scene from 1950.

Both Photos, Canadian Pacific Corporate Archives

(Above) A train of empties heads for sulphur loading on the Pecten Spur, south of Brocket, Alberta. The bridge deck was formerly the turntable at Empress, Alberta. Caboose No. 436974 brings up the rear of this October, 1973 train.   Photo by W.R. Hooper

(Below) A steam-powered passenger train is seen westbound at Fort Macleod Station in the winter of 1954.   Canadian Pacific Corporate Archives

(Above) Passengers wait for the train at Macleod Station in the early 1920's.

Glenbow-Alberta Institute

Fort Macleod and it's Railroad Dream

After the transcontinental mainline crossed the Canadian Rockies, the Canadian Pacific Railway began building branch lines to reach areas off the main route. One of these branch lines began in the early 1890's as the Calgary & Edmonton Railroad. This road opened up a huge area of choice ranching and farming country from Fort Macleod, near the U.S. border, north to the frontier city of Edmonton.

Until the railroad got to Fort Macleod, the place was just as rugged and uncivilized as its name makes it sound. The fort was home base to the region's force of Northwest Mounted Police, under the command of Colonel Macleod. Near the Fort were the reserves and camps of the Blood Indians and their close relatives, the North Peigans, both part of the large Blackfoot Confederacy. The famous "Sundance Kid," also known as Harry Longbaugh, lived in the area for a time. No troubles - he was just breaking horses to be used by the contractors for the construction of the new branch line.

Current visitors to Fort Macleod may well think the town doesn't even have a railroad, because there are no tracks or station to be seen. They can enter the town from four major directions without crossing railroad tracks. Thus they would never think of the place as one of "Western Canada's rail centers," yet, that's what plans once had envisioned.

Back in 1911 the Macleod Board of Trade waged a busy campaign to make their town the hub of no less than 10 main lines serving all of Southern Alberta. The C.P.R. already had facilities there to handle its lines east, west, and north. The Canadian Northern Railway had sent out survey parties and was apparently also going to build tracks to the town. The Grand Trunk Pacific was doing the same. Down in Montana, the Great Northern was thinking it should send a branch up to connect with all these proposed lines. And in Calgary, an enterprising group had already drawn up plans for their projected Alberta Electric Transportation Company which would run electric trains from Fort Macleod to Calgary and beyond. This got somebody else to begin talking about building a second electric line clear over into the province of Saskatchewan. The ranch lands and tree-lined river bottoms around Fort Macleod would have been dotted with factories and industries if all these traffic lines had actually been built.

By 1910 the east-west Crow's Nest branch was operating all the way to Vancouver, giving the town a direct line from ocean to ocean. In addition, the fast and prestigious "Soo Flyer" passenger train stopped there on its way from Portland and Seattle to Minneapolis and Chicago. Even when this train was cancelled in 1914, Fort Macleod continued to get good service from the Spokane Flyer, which connected Edmonton, Calgary, Crow's Nest and Spokane.

Passenger traffic through Fort Macleod ended in the 1960's and 70's with a small but efficient Dayliner service of self-propelled cars. At that time there was also talk of closing down the Macleod Sub because of its poor condition. The light freight traffic did not justify the expense of rebuilding. However, the line was saved and rebuilt with government branch line rehabilitation funds at the insistence of local ranchers and shippers.

(Above and Below) Scenes on the line west of Fort Macleod during the filming of a Canadian classic, "Cameron of the Royal Mounted." The 1920's adventure starred Gaston Glass, while supporting roles went to Indians from the nearby Peigan Reserve and to engine No. 7305, an early model 4-6-0.

Glenbow-Alberta Institute

(Above) Dawn on the prairie finds British Columbia's famous ex-C.P.R. "Royal Hudson" No. 2860 paused by the vintage station at Coalhurst, having just completed an overnight run through the Crow's Nest Pass with its special museum train. This location is now the site of CP Rail's modern Kipp yard, which replaced the aging facilities formerly at nearby Lethbridge.   AHW Photo

(Above) Royal Hudson No. 2860 becomes the first steam engine in over 20 years to cross the immense Lethbridge Viaduct in 1979. Moving slowly into the prairie sunrise, the train took nearly ten minutes to make this crossing.

AHW Photo

The Lethbridge Viaduct

The city of Lethbridge, Alberta would be noted on railway maps even if it didn't have an interesting history of narrow gauge and standard gauge railroading, or even if it wasn't an important division point and junction. It has long been fa-

mous for its spectacular example of modern engineering - the mile-long steel trestle that rates as the biggest railway bridge in North America. Approaching Lethbridge on the Southern Trans-Canada Highway No. 3, one drives from the height of the prairie far down into the Oldman River bottoms, then back up to enter the city, which is built near the prairie's edge. In the 1890's railroad engineers couldn't build their tracks up and down such steep grades, so they had to detour the C.P.R.'s Crow's Nest line far around in order to locate suitable crossings.

However, to build the line this way took more mileage than a direct route to Fort Macleod. Even worse, it needed 20 wooden bridges that required cuts, fills, steep grades, and constant maintenance. They totalled in length 2.8 miles, and were subject to washouts and fires. Loose bolts and shifting base soil often made them hazardous to cross, so that trains were required to crawl very slowly over them. After less than ten years in operation, all twenty bridges were in bad shape. Engineers estimated it would cost more than a million dollars to replace them. Survey parties were sent out to find a more practical route between Lethbridge and Fort Macleod.

Work began in 1907 to re-locate this part of the line for better operating efficiency. In addition to building the immense viaduct at Lethbridge, crews had to grade the new roadbed and build another large steel bridge over the Oldman River a few miles further west. Its length of 1,891 feet seems small compared to the 5,327 feet of the Viaduct. Before these two were built, railway men had considered some of the wooden bridges to be huge, though by comparison they were only four to six hundred feet in length, except for the one over the St. Mary River, which was a record 2,933 feet long and 65 feet high. The Lethbridge Viaduct is 314 feet high.

Statistics say that the Viaduct contains around 12,500 tons of steel. It took 645 railroad cars to bring this steel to the building site and another 250 cars to bring the rest of the materials. The bridge cost nearly 1-1/2 million dollars to build. It took 7,600 gallons of paint to give it an initial two coats.

The first problem encountered in building this challenging engineering marvel was to get accurate surveys across the deep, wide, and rugged river bottom. You can appreciate the problem all the more if you know about the strong and frequent winds that blow in this part of the country. The surveyors finally did their work with a seasoned piece of 2x4, sixteen feet long, to which they attached plumb bobs to check their levels. Wind shields had to be put in front of the plumb bobs to get steady readings.

The next problem was to build concrete foundations all the way across the difficult terrain that would be strong and accurate enough to hold this steel monster. The resulting piers had to be within 1/8 inch of each other in top measurement. The contractors used a variety of dredges, derricks, pumps, pile drivers, and other turn-of-the-century machines, backed up by a large crew of hardy workmen. Divers in old, heavy underwater suits were used to help set those of the piers that had to go where the river was running. This diffi-

cult substructure work was about completed by June, 1908, when the next major problem literally arose - the Oldman River went on a flood rampage that destroyed much of the already finished construction.

The Canadian Bridge Company of Walkerville, Ontario won the contract for erecting the steelwork. They built a large plant and material yard at the edge of the C.P.R. yard and obtained full-time use of a C.P.R. locomotive and ten flat cars. In addition, they used three large, rail-mounted vehicles for the actual construction work. The smallest of these was a crane that ran on the railway tracks.

The other two vehicles ran on rails fastened to the tops of the bridge's girder spans. They were custom-made on the spot and designed so that loaded railway cars could be run right underneath them to facilitate unloading of materials. The largest of these, known as the "traveler", had a main boom which was able to lift fifty tons. It weighed 712,000 lbs., stood 60 feet high, and took one month to build at a cost of $100,000. A mechanical wonder in its own right, it used eleven miles of cable and two 80 hp motors to lift the steel columns in place. The other vehicle that ran on the girder rails was the "riveting traveler," which was used to raise and lower cages from which workmen riveted pieces of the bridge steel together.

The great bridge was completed on June 22, 1909, and the first train to cross it did so on the same day, with some 100 dignitaries, officials, and their wives, riding on flat cars. On October 22 of the same year the other steel bridge over the Oldman River was completed, and the day after that the first train over the new shortcut ran from Macleod to Lethbridge. It consisted of an engine, caboose, and the special car "Minnedosa".

In spite of the obvious dangers entailed in building this great bridge, accidents and deaths were few. Of the three workmen who died on the job, only one fell from the bridge. The other two were suffocated by gas when they climbed down an excavated hole by one of the cement piers. Ironically, they went down to rescue two others - a boy who had climbed in and passed out, and a workman who had gone after the boy. Both of these survived. Another workman was riveting when he slipped and fell 122 feet to the snow-covered ground, below. Although the man broke both his arms, the snow saved his life.

Other people have fallen from the bridge while trespassing on it. In the 1930's a Blackfoot Indian from Montana went out towards the center and hung himself with wire fastened to one of the girders.

Another time one of a group of young boys playing on the bridge fell down to his death. In recent years a motorcycle dare-devil raced across the top of the bridge only to meet an oncoming train at the other side. He fell and was injured, while his motorcycle was crushed as the train slid over it to a stop.

(Above) The city of Lethbridge and its Viaduct, looking east from the air in 1947.

Canadian Pacific Corporate Archives

(Below) It was early 1908 when this picture was taken of the Viaduct construction. The photo shows why the huge bridge is so sturdy. The leg-beams spread way out toward the bottom, and are cross-braced many times over and together. Cement piers await more of the bridge on relatively dry land, while the contractor struggles with the wet river bottom at the foreground. Glenbow-Alberta Institute

(Above) The Crow's Nest passenger train of the mid-1950's is seen leaving Lethbridge in the early morning. Two C-liner diesel units lead the train, which consists of three lightweight and two heavy-weight cars.
Nicholas Morant Photo/Canadian Pacific Corporate Archives

(Below) Lowering the last piece into place on the Lethbridge Viaduct. In front is the big "traveler" that did the main lifting, followed by the traveler for the riveting crew, followed by a huge crane mounted on a rail car.
Glenbow-Alberta Institute

(Above) A passenger train coming up from the U.S. border to Lethbridge was stopped at the Warner water tank for this 1910 picture. No. 20 was a 2-6-0 Mogul, while No. 23 was an early 4-4-0.

Canadian Pacific Corporate Archives

(Below) Construction of the 2,033 feet long timber trestle over the St. Mary's River, near Lethbridge, on April 25th, 1898. Although it was well built, the bridge was in poor state of repair ten years later, when this part of the railroad line was replaced by the shortcut over the steel Viaduct. Floods and prairie fires posed constant threats to the wooden structure, which was 65 feet high.   K.C. Baker Collection

Early Lethbridge Railroading

Memories of Andrew Joseph Staysko

"I was born in 1890 in the coal mining country of Pennsylvania. My folks moved to Canada when I was seven. Ten years later, on April 10, 1907 I began railroading. My first job was as a wiper for the Alberta Railway & Irrigation Company. They were then running both narrow gauge and standard gauge trains out of Lethbridge. I had to look after the locomotives - wiping them down after their runs, filling their tenders with fuel and water, and preparing them for their next runs.

After five months as a wiper I was promoted to fireman, and I held that position for the next five years. I spent the last couple of those years firing the AR&I's passenger run from Lethbridge to Virden, Montana. Then, in April, 1912 the Canadian Pacific Railway took over all AR&I operations. I began working for the C.P.R. with my AR&I seniority. By that time all the AR&I trackage was standard gauge. I clearly recall my last run for the old company. It was this way:

We were coming back from the States with the Lethbridge-bound passenger train. At Stirling we picked up our train orders, and they read: 'Engineer George Alexander and Fireman Staysko, take your engine into the C.P.R. roundhouse in Lethbridge.' Up till then we had always tied up in the old, wooden, 14-stall roundhouse that was shared by the AR&I and the Great Falls & Canada Railroad. A little ways in front of it the C.P.R. had built a new roundhouse of stone, which is still being used, today.

After a short time I was set up as an engineer, so I moved to Medicine Hat for a while. Then I came back to Lethbridge and worked out of here until 1936. During the Depression I got an Irishman's promotion - that is, I went from engineer back to being a fireman. That wasn't too bad, however, since I was then the senior fireman on the roster and could take my pick of trains to work on. For seven months I fired the Kettle Valley passenger train. In those days we worked from Lethbridge clear through the Crow's Nest to Cranbrook. The pay was pretty good, since it went according to mileage, not hours worked. We usually made the 200 mile run in eight hours, while on a freight train we only did about half as good. In 1936 I transferred back to Medicine Hat, where I stayed until 1955, when I retired. At that time I was engineer on "The Canadian", which was this country's newest transcontinental passenger train, with modern equipment and diesel locomotives

I did a lot of my early running up to the Crow. For a while I was the relief engineer on the passenger train to Cranbrook. But mostly I ran freights. Those 3700's were common engines on freights from here to Crow. they weren't the best of engines around, especially for the firemen. We didn't use any pushers or helpers going west. In those days there was still a 2.2% grade at Frank, which is pretty steep. We'd go until our train stalled, then we'd have to double the train over the grade. That is, we'd take half the train over and put it on a siding, then go back for the other half. That was a helluva job, but we did get an extra ten miles pay for it. Mostly we hauled empties up to Crow for the coal.

Later, they extended the boilers on some of the 3700's and made 5200's out of them. They were 2-8-0's, but with the longer boilers they added trailing trucks and made 2-8-2's. They were like the P-1's, then, and not so hard on the firemen. I liked working on the older style light engines pretty well. Usually we got them on passenger runs; they'd roll right along with a few wooden coaches behind. They were sure a lot easier to work on than some of those big, modern engines that we got later.

The hardest part of working on passenger engines was getting them started. They had big drivers that were easy to spin. The toughest place for that was eastbound on the passenger run through the Crow, starting up at McGillivray. It took real skill with a 2600 engine to get those 10 or 12 cars stretched out properly and started evenly, considering they were sitting uphill and on a curve. This eastbound run was usually done by daylight, while the westbound run was at night. We'd lay over all day in Cranbrook, catch some sleep, and head back home the next morning.

On a typical freight trip up to Crow in those days, we'd make two turns down to Fort Macleod before they put us on an eastbound freight clear back to Lethbridge. We'd be gone from home 5 or 6 days, and we'd look like hoboes with our beards and dirty clothing by the time we got back. Working on diesel-powered passenger trains at the end was a much different thing from those rugged steam days."

(Above) Built in 1906 and doubled in 1910 the Lethbridge station seen in this 1909 photo still stands, although the scene itself looks totally different. The name of the town used to be Coaldale, but in 1885 it was renamed in honor of William Lethbridge, the first president of the North-West Coal & Navigation Co. Many people today mistakenly think the town was named for its record bridge, instead.
(Below) The C.P.R. yard at Lethbridge not long after the great Viaduct was opened. It can barely be seen to the left of the smoke-stack, by the coaling tower and roundhouse. Beyond the switcher, at left, is part of the town. Some of the buildings are still standing. In the yard are a variety of old freight cars most of them made of wood. There are two cars filled with coal, several gondolas full of firewood, and a string of livestock cars in the foreground.   Both Photos, Glenbow-Alberta Institute

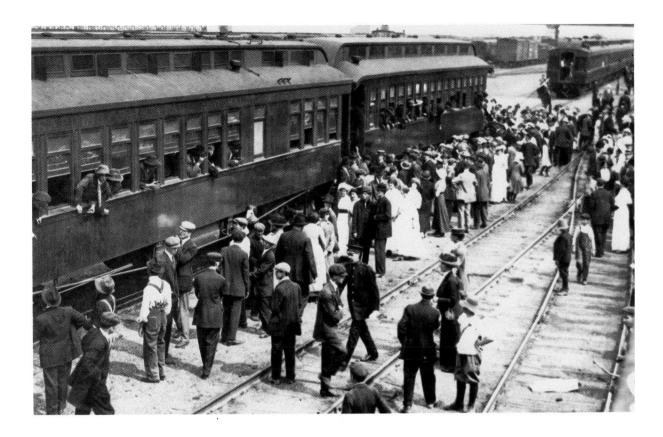

(Above) A crowd is gathered around cars of the "Soo Flyer" at the station in Lethbridge during the final months of the train's operation, just before the start of the first world war. The Ninth Street Bridge, in back, still carries Lethbridge traffic.

(Below) Engine No. 592 gets ready to head out of town with Rotary Snowplow No. 4248, while a freight waits nearby to follow behind. The C.P.R. built eight of these steam-powered plows in 1888 and bought another one from the U.S. in 1907. All were eventually scrapped.

Both Photos/Glenbow-Alberta Institute

Lethbridge in the Forties

By Elmer Penrose

"My first paid trip as a fireman was aboard the midnight yard switcher here in Lethbridge. That was the lowest job on the line-up. We had the number 6809 - a little six-wheeled (0-6-0) switcher with a slope backed tender that just had enough fuel and water for working around the yards. We called these the "Mother Hubbard type", because they had a cab that went half way up to the front of the small boiler. If I wanted to see the engineer I had to stand up high enough so I could look over the boiler. To fire the thing I had to go back on a little catwalk to the boiler head, where I could scoop coal into the firebox opening.

This first night aboard that little switcher I had Ernie Fullylove for an engineer. He was a nice man to work with as a beginner, he didn't get impatient with me. I still recall that he used to smoke his cigarettes with a long cigarette holder.

Along about three in the morning we stopped for some lunch and Ernie told me to put some water on. Now, I had only made three student trips before this, because the company was in a hurry to get more firemen. On those three trips we always stopped for water at regular water tanks, where you lowered the big spout down to your tender. We had never stopped at a standpipe like there was in the Lethbridge yard then. The water tank was nearby, but this pipe just stood up by itself.

The engineer spotted the engine by the water pipe and then said he would make us a pot of tea while I put the water in. When I got up on the tender I couldn't figure out how to get the spout over to me, and when I finally did then I couldn't figure out how to make it go down close to the hatch so it wouldn't spill all over. I pulled on different things, and then I pulled harder, and suddenly the water opened up and went all over and flooded the engineer and his tea kettle. He let out a holler. I got it shut off, and then I tried to work it once more, but the same thing happened again, until finally I got it figured out.

It didn't take long to learn the main tricks of railroading, like how to get the water spout to the tender. But after I fired for a while I got called into the Army, so I didn't get back to the C.P.R. till after World War II. Then I worked steadily out of Lethbridge, going in all directions. We were proud of our work and we liked working for the Company. I remember how good it felt to be aboard one of our clean and well-cared for C.P.R. engines when we went down to Coutts, at the U.S. border. The Great Northern crew would meet us from the other side, and they would look at us with envy from their own grimy engines.

I worked up to Crow on freight and passenger trains. Going out of Lethbridge on the westbound, our first stop for passengers was at Coalhurst. Next came Monarch and Pearce, which were flag stops. Then we made good time, stopping again at Fort Macleod, Brocket, Pincher, Cowley,

and Lundbreck, where we took water. Next was Hillcrest and then Frank, where we got coal and water, both. Then we went on to Blairmore, Coleman, and Summit. There was no station at Summit, just a tool shed and a sign. Inside the tool shed there were two lanterns - one white and one green - and a set of instructions. The passenger had to light the lanterns and set them out on the platform for a train to stop. One of the trainmen put them away, afterwards. Passenger trains usually went through here at night, but if it was daytime the passenger put out green and white flags, instead. At Crow we changed crews and rested.

One time I was firing for Engineer Parfitt, as we rolled through Coleman. At the station the engineer leaned out and got the orders, read them, and passed them over to me. The order said, "No. 5149 meet No. 5152 coming east at Summit." Well, we were on No. 5152, but we were going west. I told Parfitt, so he stopped the train and sent the head brakeman back for a correction. Somebody had made a mistake, was all, but such a mistake could have resulted in a bad accident. After that time, Engineer Parfitt had a higher regard of me.

It wasn't always easy to catch those train order hoops, like in a high wind storm or during a blizzard. If you missed it, you had to stop your train and send somebody back for it, and that didn't go over too well with the superintendents. Once I was running a diesel on the head of a freight through Canmore. The fireman and head brakeman were both asleep. I saw the clear signal from a distance, but I missed the order board telling me to pick up the train orders. Next thing I knew, there was the station and an operator with a train order hoop ready, with me going 45 miles an hour! I leaned out and tried for it, but I was going too fast, so I had to stop the whole train and send the brakeman back.

One time they had quite a mess on their hands up at Crow's Nest. Somebody left a valve open on that big fuel tank that served the engines, and the whole roundhouse area got flooded with oil. They decided to dump cinders around the tracks to soak some of it up. They took an engine and went to the cinder pit to get some gondolas filled with cinders from the locomotives. These cars were standing in a deep pool of oil. When they were pulled out, they oiled the tracks all the way up, but nobody noticed it. After they got them all dumped, they went to put the empty cars back down in the cinder pit, but once they got in that oiled section of the track they couldn't stop, so they piled up that string of empty gons all over the cinder track.

Another time I was headed from Crow's Nest back to Lethbridge, and my number was nearly called. I was the fireman, and we had a 5100 on the head of a long freight. At Blairmore we got held up, and it turned out to be a long wait. There was no engine waiting at Blairmore and we couldn't go further east without a pusher. We figured it had been sent down to Pincher to help No. 11 past Frank. That was standard procedure when the passenger train was heavy. After a while I left the engine and went to a nearby cafe to eat, figuring I could hurry back before the helper could uncouple from No. 11 and hook on to our train. But I finished eating and went back up to the cab and there was still nothing. Then the engineer told me that there was a wreck up ahead.

It turned out that a 5200 with another heavy freight had plunged into a washout after a flash flood, just a little ways out of Lundbreck. All three men aboard the engine were killed. Their train stopped on a curve, so the rear brakeman walked forward to find out the trouble. He brought a lantern and an extra air hose, thinking the air line had broken somewhere along the train. When he got around the curve there was nothing - no train, no engine, and no sound. The steam domes had been sheared off the engine during the crash and she was dead, the cars piled on top of her. It was lucky that No. 11 happened to be behind this freight, and not ahead.

We spent a week on the west side of the wreck, until they got the line back into operation. That first night we ended up making a light run down there with just our caboose. The engineer and I helped pull the rope that brought the dead engineer up out of his cab. The two others had been washed downstream and weren't found until later. We were pretty queasy about that job.

We spent most of the week hauling flatcar loads of building materials down to the wreck site. There was only one hook on the job - the steam crane from Lethbridge. I think the one from Cranbrook was busy somewhere else. We were paid for eight out of every twenty-four hours away from home, in addition to the time we actually worked.

That was a bad spring for wrecks, anyway. There were two wrecks down at Cowley, not long before. In each of them two engines turned over. In the first one the engineer said that he lost his air going down into the bridge, west of Cowley, so he couldn't stop his train from sideswiping another freight just going into the siding at Cowley.

The hook didn't even get back to Lethbridge from this collision when it was given orders to return to Cowley. Another engineer had overlooked his orders and wasn't prepared to stop for a meet when he got to Cowley, so he hit the opposing freight, and both his engines went down. I was working on the engine next to the hook, for this job. When the steam crane got one of the engines about half way up it ran out of water, so they had to hurry and hook up its steam pipes to the steam dome of our engine to keep working.

Diesels sure changed things on the railway for me, so that I ended up leaving. The first diesel came into Lethbridge with a freight train about a week after New Year's Day, 1952, although they ran gas-electric cars for passengers on some of the branch lines in the 1940's. We called this one-car train "The Galloping Goose". For a while it ran to Coutts, then it went to Cardston and Glenwood. It held about 50 passengers, along with baggage and express. Later it was replaced by the Dayliner. The first diesel-powered passenger train into Lethbridge came in on June 26, 1953. Jack Scott was the engineer, and the Mayor of Lethbridge went out to greet the train.

My first trip running a diesel came one night when somebody booked off sick from the passenger run east out of Lethbridge. At that time Trains 11 and 12 were regularly worked by No. 4065 which was the original of the C-Liner diesels. I saw it come through as the "City of Kingston", when it was a demonstrator model from the Canadian Locomotive Works, at Kingston, Ontario. The C.P.R. got 16 of them and they all worked out of Lethbridge.

In those days they always sent a pilot out with the crew running a diesel for the first time - usually the road foreman of engines. But this night they didn't have anybody available, so they sent the electrician out with me, and he didn't know much more about it than I did. But we had a nice trip, when we got it all figured out. There was a thunder storm out on the prairie, and it sure was a sight to watch through those wide windows way up high, in front."

Below) No. 724 was typical of the many D-10 Class Ten-Wheeler (4-6-0) engines that worked light freight and passenger service out of Lethbridge. This photo was taken in June, 1946.   W.C. Whittaker

(Above) A 1950's view of the Lethbridge roundhouse taken from the water tower. Note the Lethbridge Viaduct in far distance.
John Poulsen Photo

(Below) Fast engine No. 3001 was a regular on the "Chinook" out of Calgary. She fell into the turntable during a short career around Lethbridge in 1942. Engineer J.L. Middleton had her on a train when the air compressor failed, which left no engine brakes and no reverse. He brought the train in with only the train brakes, then ran the engine carefully into the shop track. The wiper later went to move her ahead, but forgot to line up the turntable first. Once he got started there was no way to stop. A lot of sweat, plus the Big Hook in back, were needed to pull No. 3001 back out.
John Poulsen Collection

(Above) Pacific-type (4-6-2) No. 2384 next to the cinder pit in Lethbridge during the final seasons of steam, about 1957.
(Below) Gas-electric car No. 9003 leaves the roundhouse for a branch line passenger run out of Lethbridge in the late Forties.

Both Photos, John Poulsen

(Above) The last steam-powered train to enter Lethbridge in revenue service came from Medicine Hat in January 1959 behind Mikado No. 5219 and is seen here near the station.
(Below) The last revenue train to cross the Lethbridge Viaduct behind steam is seen here about the same time.

Both Photos, John Poulsen

(Above) The big steel water tower survived by the Lethbridge roundhouse until both were torn down with the closing of the yard in 1983. Here's the last steam engine to take a drink from its spout - No. 2860 in 1979.

(Below) Lethbridge, in the final seasons of having a downtown railway yard. In the foreground is "Extra Speeno Rail Grinding Service Train East," slowly moving over tracks that are being tested for wear, then given a grinding accordingly, all usually in one pass.   Both Photos, AHW

Train Time at the Station

By Hattie I. Chester
(From *Lethbridge Herald*, March 11, 1972)

"We used to set our clock by the train, it varied so little in time. When we heard the distant 'Whoo-oo-oo' of the whistle, we'd look out to see the train wind into sight and quickly disappear around the next bend... across the fields east of our house. We always knew, too, where to look for the smoke of the approaching train, just where the grade was a little steeper and a little more power was needed.

There were so many interesting things about travelling on a train ... We never knew whom we might meet or what might happen. From the moment we climbed the steps to the station platform and entered the waiting room with its bare, shiny benches along the walls our hearts beat faster in anticipation.

At the wicket, the agent peered at you over his glasses, 'Going to Lethbridge? Round trip?' And you felt important. You took the little piece of cardboard and sat down. Probably there were two or three neighbors or acquaintances there and the agent joined in the conversation, poking his face close to the wicket bars. Maybe there was a stranger and somebody tried to get him into the conversation and get him around to indicating what his business in town had been.

Then the whistle of the train sounded as it emerged from the cut north of town and blew for the crossing. Everyone hurried outside and tried to place himself where he thought the train might stop so he'd be first on and get the choice of any vacant seats. Entering the long coach with its faint smell of disinfectant or moth-proofing, whatever it was, we looked around for the best seat available, by the window if possible. We had probably seen the landscape fifty times, but always wanted to watch it move along nevertheless...

The engine belched and coughed, gave a big 'chuff' and a jerk, and we were under way. The conductor came and took one end of your ticket, and gave the rest back for the return trip. You stored it safely away in some snug part of your purse, and took stock of your fellow travellers, mostly those from adjacent small towns going to the city for the afternoon.

In a few minutes the Newsy came along, carrying a large basket containing magazines, chocolate bars, gum, fruit and peanuts. He called his wares as he moved slowly along, 'Chewing gum, Gripes, MAG-zines, oranges, PAY-nuts,' and sometimes, 'Sandwiches.'...It was seldom that he reappeared from the other direction, and I used to wonder if he got off at one of the other stations and returned to his place in the baggage car, or whether he rode the rest of the way on the engine, after treating the crew to some of his wares. When the train no longer carried a Newsy, I missed his gravely voice and weird pronunciations.

It was interesting watching the people on the platform in other small towns, some saying good-bye to visitors from a distance perhaps, others, like ourselves, going in for an afternoon of shopping, or maybe a show. So the train rambled on through the countryside, through a deep cut here, on a grade a few feet above there, stopping at Coalhurst to switch to the main line. Then we were at the high level bridge across the coulee and the Oldman River. It was never a casual experience going across that. Looking down and seeing the coulees spread out far below, then the thread of the river, and the road and traffic bridge, cars almost like match-box toys, a long way down.

The conductor called, 'Lethbridge! Everybody change!' We were there. The engine stood puffing and blowing as if trying to cool off after its labors, but we didn't give it much thought as we scurried for the station door, and whatever destination we sought.

Going home in the dusk or dark of the evening was more adventuresome still, especially if it was winter, and the railway yards full of the fog of white steam as one boarded the train. And as it puffed and wailed its way along, billows of white smoke or steam sailed by the darkened windows, and when it stopped at a station, there was a great rush of escaping steam, and clouds of vapor mingling with the smoke as the engine panted to be on its way.

One often had small contretemps of some kind, too, on a train journey. One dark night, the train stopped at a station, and I was sure it was mine. I hurried out, but found the steel platform over the steps hadn't been raised. I wasn't in the forward coach that night as it had been full when I got on, and it was possible that the conductor had forgotten that there was another local passenger. There wasn't time to rush through the next car (as I thought), so I went to the edge of the steel lid and jumped down, bundles and all. As I looked about me at the deserted station I realized that I had alighted at the town next to ours. I grasped the edge of the steel platform and pulled myself up, fearing every second that the train would take off with me dangling there. Luckily it was dark and nobody was about to witness my indignity."

(Above) Consolidation No. 3608 leads a southbound freight at Claresholm, on the Macleod Sub, in the 1940's.

R.V. Nixon Photo

(Below) A caboose hop passes Claresholm station southbound in 1979. The stone building was moved here from Calgary in 1912 aboard flat cars. It now serves as a local museum. Claresholm was first reached by tracks of the Calgary & Edmonton Railway in 1891.

AHW Photo

(Left) A pair of GP-9's and a wooden caboose were part of this southbound way freight serving towns and grain elevators between Calgary and Fort Macleod in June 1979. Both,
AHW Photos

(Below) High River, Alberta shows how it got its name. During the flood of May 1942, a train of ballast has stopped at the water tank, which is now the site of the High River Railway Museum, which includes examples of restored trains. Centerpiece of that museum is the town's stone station (just out of sight to the left), brought from Calgary in 1911, and similar to the one at Claresholm. The two buildings had previously made up Calgary's downtown station.
Glenbow-Alberta Institute

(Above) Ranching country around Okotoks, Alberta was served by this sizable wooden CPR station until it burned to the ground. A brick replacement remains today as a historical landmark.
(Below) The morning passenger train from Calgary to Lethbridge is seen at the busy station of Vulcan in 1915, with trim 4-6-0 No. 2101 in the lead.   Both Photos, Glenbow-Alberta Institute

(Above) Along the same line between Calgary and Lethbridge is Barons, Alberta, whose two-story station is seen here in 1910. At left is station agent, A.E. McDermott, with bowler hat, pipe, and a badge on his chest.   Glenbow-Alberta Institute

(Below) Grain elevators and corrals with loading chutes were part of every prairie station setting, such as this typical scene in 1949.   Canadian Pacific Corporate Archives

• CALGARY •

Calgary-Alt. 3,388 ft. Pop. 4,500. 2264 miles from Montreal. The most important, as well as the handsomest, place between Brandon and Vancouver, has recently been created a city. It is charmingly situated on a hill-girt plateau, overlooked by the white peaks of the Rockies. It is the center of the trade of the great ranching country and the chief source of supply for the mining districts in the mountains beyond. Excellent building materials" abound in the vicinity. Lumber is largely made here from logs floated down Bow River. From Calgary, a branch line runs north to Edmonton on the Saskatchewan and south to Macleod, thus throwing open a new and vast country which is annually attracting settlers in large numbers. Calgary is an important station of the Mounted Police, and a post of the Hudson's Bay Company."

From a C.P.R. Tour Guide of the 1880's

(Above) an early-day train with wood burning 4-4-0 No. 98 is seen stopped at Calgary's station in the 1880's. The first station was only a boxcar.
(Below) Calgary's third station was this substantial building made with stone from Pincher Creek. Cut in half and moved on flatcars, this structure eventually became two stations, one at Claresholm, the other High River. Both are standing today and in use as museums. Both Photos, Glenbow-Alberta Institute

(Above) The original wooden roundhouse at Alyth yard in Calgary in the 1890's, with shop crews and 4-6-0 No. 465 nosed onto the turntable. Glenbow-Alberta Institute

(Below) High-stepping 4-6-0 No. 2008 arrives in Calgary with a two-car branch line passenger train sometime in the early 1920's. Paterson-George Collection

(Above) Looking west at downtown Calgary in about 1920, with the fourth C.P.R. station (in foreground), backed by the Paliser Hotel, both fronting on the passenger yard.

Canadian Pacific Corporate Archives

(Below) Looking east on 8th Avenue, with a streetcar of the Calgary Municipal Railway running through what is now a pedestrian mall.

Glenbow-Alberta Institute

(Above) Calgary greets the Stampeders football team, returning home aboard a special train after winning Canada's 1949 Grey Cup. Parade cars wait to take the party further.
(Below) Two streetcars pass under the CPR bridge and tracks over 1st Street S.W. in October 1911.

Memories of Calgary Area Railroading

By Clayton Harris

"On the 15th of January, 1920, I was working in a pool-room setting pins and so forth. The locomotive foreman came over from the roundhouse and said he was desperate for a man and could I go to work right then. I didn't want to walk out on my boss at the pool hall, but he said to go ahead, so I hired on with the C.P.R.

As locomotive watchman at Banff I had to look after any engines left there. My usual job was to take care of the way-freight engine, to keep its fire going during the night and to grease it up. This train came to Banff from Calgary every Monday. On the way they would stop and coal up at Canmore. I only had to shovel the coal forward in the tender. On Tuesday morning they would head back to Calgary. On Wednesday they would make a trip from Calgary to Lake Louise, and lay over there. So I had to go up to Lake Louise to meet them, and then back to Banff the next day, while they went on to Calgary. On Friday they would make another trip to Banff.

Whenever they had a work train around Banff I had to look after their engines, too. One night I had seven locomotives to take care of, and I sure was kept busy! The work trains used mostly 3800's, sometimes 3500's, and later 3600's. Towards the end they even used P-12-8-2's on work trains, but for most of their years they worked on through freight. On each engine I would fill the lubricators, grease the side rods with a gun, and clean the fires out. I just dumped the ashes right on the tracks and then sprayed water from the tender on them, so the ties wouldn't burn. The section men would clean up the ashes the next morning.

There was a turntable just east of the station, at Banff, and sometimes I had to turn engines on it. That was a tricky job, because the engine had to be balanced just right so I could turn the table by hand. Across the tracks from the station was a bunk house and an ice house.

At the east end of the station there were three long garden tracks, and on the west end there were two which ran nearly to the road crossing. There were a lot of tourist trains in those days, and they often left cars parked on these garden tracks for two or three days, while the tourists visited around the Banff area. Brewster buses would meet them at the station and drive them around. Sometimes these trains had two or three hundred people with them. Some would stay in the Pullman cars and some would stay up at the Banff Springs Hotel. Special tourist trains used to come up from the States with their own cars. Some trains brought special cars to Banff as part of these popular Circle Tours from the Pacific Coast to Chicago. For instance, C.P.R.'s trains 13 and 14 were generally made up of cars that came up from the Soo Line, through Moose Jaw. We also had Trains 1 & 2 going east and west; Trains 3 and 4, the "Do-minion;" Trains 5 and 6, the overflow train that carried mail cars and express; and Trains 7 and 8, which we called "the rich people's trains", because they carried first class equipment and got special service.

The garden tracks were also for privately-owned cars, of which there were quite a number in those days. For instance, the Crane family, who have big factories making plumbing fixtures and so forth, had a son who was allergic to the climate in the States, where they lived. So his father brought him up to Banff in a private car. They'd often stay for 2 months. He was a fine man, that boy's father, and friendly to everyone. Some of these people weren't, of course.

You could even rent a private car from the C.P.R. and stay in it, at Banff or wherever you wanted. They would hook the cars up to steam and water pipes.

These trains that stayed in Banff for several days left their engine hooked up for steam, which they used for heating. The engine crews would stay at the bunkhouse, and I would look after their engine at nights. They looked after it in the daytime and got paid regular wages for it. It was easy money for them especially when they got oil burning engines.

I remember when Buck Crump was shop foreman in Field. There was a baseball team, there, and he was the second baseman. There was another team at Golden, and one time they came up to play Field. Fireman Art Campbell went to check on him and found him filling out company reports. He told Crump: 'C'mon, throw these papers in the trash - what do you think you're gonna be, vice president someday?' And here he became president, and a good one. The men were glad to work for him. We knew that he didn't expect too much of us - just an honest day's work!

If we came into Field on a regular run we got to stay at the bunkhouse for free. We'd eat at the YMCA, then rest up for our return trip. But when we got stationed at Field we'd stay at the "Y" for eight or ten dollars a month, and eat there. Some of the boys ate in the Chinese restaurant up the hill, after they went up to the 'Ten-cent Store'. That's where they had a few glasses of 10 cent beer.

There was a train that got away on its engineer coming down the Big Hill, after I started working. It was during the Depression. They had a heavy train, with a 5800 engine, heading towards Yoho. The brakes were at full set, and the brakeman went up and set some hand brakes, but they still couldn't slow her down, so the brakeman jumped off at Yoho and told the dispatcher the problem. The dispatcher got the track cleared ahead, but the train never went faster than about 20 mph, so it didn't derail. It finally slowed to a stop on the level at Field. It was a wheat train, headed west. That sort of thing didn't happen much anymore by my time but it happened often in the early years.

Going west from Calgary into the Rockies was pretty hard going back when we had hand-fired coal burners. As a fireman I would pretty well strip the tender empty between Calgary and Canmore, and again between there and Stephen. But the mountain water was good for steaming. In the winter I would have to watch my engines so that the hoses to the tenders didn't freeze up. In the days before water pumps, all the engines had inspirators with their steam pipes. A little rod by the side of the inspirator allowed hot steam to go back to the tender through the water pipe to keep things thawed. But I would have to watch out that I didn't get things too warm, because the injector wouldn't pick up water from the tender if it was too warm.

In 1942 I wrote up my engineer's exam. There were 46 men in our class, because they hadn't written up any engineers during the Depression years, so the war caught them short. The government needed men to work on the Northern Alberta Railway, which runs north out of Edmonton.

When I came back to Calgary from the N.A.R. I was the youngest man on the spare board as an engineer. At that time there was a passenger train out of Calgary each morning to Fort Macleod and Lethbridge, via Aldersyde and Claresholm. Twenty minutes after it left there was another one down to Coalhurst and Lethbridge. The first one used Calgary crews, while the other one had firemen both ways from Lethbridge, and one engineer from there while the other engineer was from Calgary. This regular Calgary engineer got tired of the job and it was advertised as vacant. It was a good run, so I didn't think much about it. But the day before it closed I put in my application to bid on it and I got it. I was the youngest engineer to hold a regular passenger run, and I kept it all summer. That was a good job, one of the best I've had.

I used to bring along my lunch to cut down on expenses. We had a 24-hour layover in Lethbridge, during which I stayed at the bunkhouse for free. We generally had engine No. 1239, which was a nice engine. She had a new type of injector for putting the water in the boiler. I studied up on how it worked, and I used to instruct the firemen on it. Finally some of the older engineers wanted to bid on the run,

so they got some slight change made to open it up for bid, and of course I got bumped off by a much older man.

After that good job I went back to the spare board. Over the years I pretty well worked every kind of run there was. Toughest were the snowplows, because you couldn't see where you were going. Working on pusher engines out of Field was pretty good work. We'd be on duty for 12 hours and get paid for 150 miles. We'd work from Field to Lake Louise, and sometimes make a few trips between Lake Louise and the summit of Stephen, if there were several trains close behind each other. We would turn our engine at the Wye at Lake Louise. When we started to get short of fuel and water we'd run back down to Field. Pusher service wasn't hard work for the fireman, either. We'd make the short run uphill, then coast back downhill. One time I worked on a pusher for a train of 80 or 90 empties going back to the prairies for wheat. We had two engines on the head-end, another in the middle, and a fourth one on the back.

Sometimes I even worked up to Crow's Nest, out of Lethbridge. The steep grade at Frank made tough work with a heavy load, especially if you had a poor engine. That wasn't a high revenue run - a lot of shipments were the company's own coal, so the Crow was famous for having poor equipment. Often they got engines that were ready for the scrap line. When we were on the passenger train into Lethbridge and we saw a guy getting in from the Crow's Nest, we'd say: 'There's one of those tough birds down off the Crow.' You had to be tough to handle the work.

Sometimes when I got laid over long enough in the mountains I would go out for a hike, and pick fresh flowers to bring home for my wife. Sometimes my fireman would come along with me. Up at the Great Divide the passenger trains used to stop so that the tourists could get a look. One of the trainmen would give a little talk about it, and in mixed company he would say, 'from here you can spit into both oceans.' If the passengers were all men he would say something else you could do into both oceans. They had a little canal by the tracks were you could see the waters heading east and west. A vendor would sell postcards that tourists could mail from there."

(Below) A westbound freight leaves Calgary in the 1940's behind mighty 2-10-2 No. 5813, bound for Banff and the Rockies beyond. Canadian Pacific Corporate Archives

(Above) The Palliser Hotel has long been a notable backdrop for photos of CPR trains stopped at the passenger station in Calgary. Here's Selkirk No. 5929 waiting to head west with the "Dominion" in 1946.

R.V. Nixon Photo

(Below) This interior view of the Ogden Shops was taken in September, 1945. It shows a locomotive being lifted by the 250-ton crane which was then the largest of its kind in Canada.

Canadian Pacific Corporate Archives

(Above) Portrait of pride, Pacific (4-6-4) No. 2342 gleams in the afternoon light of Calgary in September 1928.

R.V. Nixon Photo

(Below) This classic shot of passenger train service in the 1920's shows CPR 4-6-0 No. 585 leading Train No. 4 "Toronto Express" eastbound at Calgary.

C.R. Littlebury Photo

INDEX

(Above) C.P.R. steam days in downtown Calgary. The first and second sections of Train No. 7 wait beside the Palliser Hotel to depart westbound behind a pair of "Selkirk" 2-10-4's in 1941.

G.L. Moorhouse Photo

Bibliography

Affleck, E.L., STERNWHEELERS, SANDBARS AND SWITCHBACKS. Vancouver: The Alexander Nicolls Press, 1973.

Baillie-Grohman, W.A., FIFTEEN YEAR'S SPORT AND LIFE IN THE HUNTING GROUNDS OF WESTERN AMERICA AND BRITISH COLUMBIA. London: Horace Cox, 1900.

Bain, Donald M., CANADIAN PACIFIC IN THE ROCKIES (Volumes One, Two & Three.) Calgary: The Calgary Group of the British Railway Modellers of North America, 1978-1979.

Berton, Pierre, THE LAST SPIKE. Toronto: McClelland and Stewart, 1971.

Bowman, R.F.P., RAILWAYS IN SOUTHERN ALBERTA. Lethbridge: Whoop-Up Country Chapter, Historical Society of Alberta, Occasional Paper No. 4, 1973.

Johnston, Alex, THE C.P. RAIL HIGH LEVEL BRIDGE AT LETHBRIDGE. Lethbridge: Whoop-Up Country Chapter, Historical Society of Alberta, Occasional Paper No. 7, 1977.

Lavallee, Omer, 1969. "Up, over and under, THE SPANNER, Vol. 8, No. 5, p. 8.

CANADIAN RAIL, The monthly journal of the Canadian Railroad Historical Association. Issues consulted: No. 218 "Coal to Japan," by Robert A. Loat; No. 275 "The Big Hill and the Mountain Section," by Thomas Huntley Crump; No. 294 "McGillivray and the Loop," by Patrick Webb.